Images of the Sign

IMAGES OF THE SIGN

Semiotic Consciousness in the Novels of
BENITO PÉREZ GALDÓS

Akiko Tsuchiya

University of Missouri Press
Columbia and London

5   4   3   2   1   94   93   92   91   90

Library of Congress Cataloging-in-Publication Data
Tsuchiya, Akiko, 1959–
     Images of the sign : semiotic consciousness in the novels
of Benito Pérez Galdós / Akiko Tsuchiya.
        p.   cm.
     Includes bibliographical references.
     ISBN 0–8262–0745–6 (alk. paper)
     1. Pérez Galdós, Benito, 1843–1920—Criticism and
interpretation. 2. Semiotics and literature. I. Title.
PQ6555.Z5T78   1990
863'.5—dc20   90–37375
                                                              CIP

∞™ This paper meets the requirements of the
American National Standard for Permanence of Paper
for Printed Library Materials, Z39.48, 1984.

Designer: Darin M. Powell
Typesetter: Connell-Zeko Type & Graphics
Printer: Thomson-Shore, Inc.
Binder: Thomson-Shore, Inc.
Type face: Baskerville

This book was brought to publication with the generous
assistance of the Program for Cultural Cooperation Between
Spain's Ministry of Culture and United States' Universities.

For Jonathan

Contents

Acknowledgments   *ix*

Introduction   *1*

1. Maxi and the Signs of Madness   *13*

2. The Myth of the Natural Sign in
   El doctor Centeno   *35*

3. The Struggle for Autonomy in *Tristana*   *55*

4. *La incógnita* and the Enigma of Writing   *81*

5. History as Language in the First Series
   of the *Episodios nacionales*   *106*

Conclusion   *129*

Works Cited   *135*

Index   *143*

Acknowledgments

This book began as a doctoral dissertation at Cornell University. I am deeply grateful to John W. Kronik, who not only first introduced me to the works of Galdós, but also enthusiastically guided this project from beginning to end. The final product owes much to his exigence and meticulousness as a reader. I would also like to thank Mary Gaylord and Kathleen Vernon, the other members of my dissertation committee, for their careful reading of the manuscript at various stages of its elaboration. They offered many valuable suggestions from different perspectives. My colleague Maria Cooks generously agreed to proofread my English translations, and Rick Boland, of the University of Missouri Press, did a wonderful job in copyediting the manuscript. My greatest debt, finally, is to my husband Jonathan Mayhew, who was always willing to engage in Galdosian dialogue with me and who unfailingly provided me with the encouragement and moral support necessary to complete this project.

Portions of this book have been published previously as the following articles: "Maxi and the Signs of Madness: Reading as Creation in *Fortunata y Jacinta*," *Hispanic Review* 56 (1988): 53–71; "The Struggle for Autonomy in Galdós's *Tristana*," *MLN* 104 (1989): 330–50; "*La incógnita* and the Enigma of Writing: Manolo Infante's Interpretive Struggle," *Hispanic Review* 57 (1989): 335–56; and "History as Language in the First Series of the *Episodios Nacionales:* The Literary Self-Creation of Gabriel de Araceli," *Anales Galdosianos* (in press).

Images of the Sign

The eye does not see things but images of things that mean other things.

—Italo Calvino, *Invisible Cities*

Introduction

Il n'y a pas d'art qui ne désigne son masque du doigt.

(There is no art that does not point to its own mask.)

—Roland Barthes

Studies of Benito Pérez Galdós's novels from contemporary critical perspectives are becoming increasingly prevalent in a field that, until the most recent decade, has been dominated by biographical, sociological, and historical criticism. A number of *galdosistas*, among them John W. Kronik, Ricardo Gullón, and Germán Gullón, followed by Kay Engler, Diane Urey, and a few others, have directed Galdosian studies toward a new critical terrain. Developments in modern literary theory, which have demanded a redefinition of the notion of *realism* and of the novelistic genre itself, have provided the critical tools necessary for these scholars to reevaluate Galdós's works from a new perspective.

Roland Barthes, whose ideas have been fundamental to the evolution of mainstream semiotics and of subsequent post-structuralist movements, has repeatedly affirmed the essentially linguistic nature of all literary texts: "simultaneously an insistent proposition of meaning and a stubbornly fugitive meaning, literature is indeed only a *language*, i.e., a system of signs; its being is not in its message but in this 'system.'" In the same essay, he declares that the object of criticism is "not 'the world' but a discourse, the discourse of someone else."[1] Given this perspective, the realist novel, as an example of one such "discourse," needs to be reexamined as a product of linguistic and literary conventions, regardless of the extent to which it conceals (or reveals) its condition as artifice. In her discussion of metafictional texts, Linda Hutcheon challenges the notion of realism as "product mimesis" alone and insists that auto-representation, the text's representation of its own diegetic and linguistic processes, is essential to the concept of realism.[2] She postulates

---

1. *Critical Essays*, 259–60, 258.
2. Hutcheon defines the "mimesis of product" as the theoretical basis of "tradi-

1

the concept of "mimesis of process" to characterize those novels that thematize the creative functions of the reader within the texts.[3]

Many works of nineteenth-century realism, from *Madame Bovary* (1857) to *La Regenta* (1884), show to a varying degree an awareness of their narrative and linguistic processes.[4] The creative acts of characters such as Emma Bovary, Ana Ozores, and Víctor Quintanar reflect the struggle of the realist novel to define itself ontologically as a linguistic construct. Linguistic self-reflection similarly occupies a central place in the novels of Galdós, in which narrators, characters, and readers constantly and obsessively engage in the acts of interpretation and creation. People, things, and verbal enunciations become explicit objects of semiotic meditation for these subjects.

"Semiotics," Robert Innis writes, is "the doctrine or general theory of signs. To put it bluntly, it deals with meanings and messages in all their forms and in all their contexts."[5] As general as this definition of semiotics may seem, it summarizes the common basis of a theory that found its first systematic formulations in Saussure's structural linguistics and Peirce's pragmatist philosophy. Later, in the second half of the twentieth century, semiotics developed into a methodological tool for disciplines as varied as anthropology, zoology, and literary criticism. Saussure's model has been most influential in literary criticism, probably because it privileges language among all the sign systems.[6] "The

---

tional realism," which, by denying the existence of conventions, holds literature to be a direct imitation of an extratextual reality: "The reader is required to identify the products being imitated—characters, actions, settings—and recognize their similarity to those in empirical reality, in order to validate their literary worth" (*Narcissistic Narrative: The Metafictional Paradox*, 38).

3. Ibid, 39.

4. Hutcheon makes note of those critics who have interpreted *Madame Bovary* as "an allegory of the power of language and literature" (ibid., 38). For readings of *La Regenta* as a self-reflexive text, see Germán Gullón, *La novela como acto imaginativo*, 123–47, and Stephanie Sieburth, "Interpreting *La Regenta*: Coherence vs. Entropy." Gullón views the discursive function of Clarín's narrator as a sign of the novel's reflexivity (*La novela*, 142). Sieburth demonstrates how the dialogue between the multiplicity of "mutually referential [textual] fragments" in *La Regenta* constitutes a commentary on the novel's own workings ("Interpreting *La Regenta*," 283).

5. Introduction to *Semiotics: An Introductory Anthology*, ed. Robert E. Innis, vii.

6. "Signs that are wholly arbitrary realize better than the others the ideal of the semiological process; that is why language, the most complex and universal of all systems of expression, is also the most characteristic; in this sense linguistics can become the master-pattern for all branches of semiology although language is only

project for semiotics," Eco says, is to "study the whole of culture, and thus to view an immense range of objects and events as signs."[7] The literary text becomes a privileged object of such a study, since all "objects and events" within it are specifically linguistic signs.[8] My own critical framework, which takes language per se to be the basic model for the various semiotic systems within the literary text, owes much to Saussure's ideas. Rather than applying a preformulated theory to literary texts, however, I hope to make eclectic use of general semiotic theory as a heuristic tool for my analyses, ultimately allowing the texts themselves to guide my theoretical orientation.

One of the essential characteristics of language as a semiotic system is its ability to reflect upon itself as a sign.[9] This metalinguistic commentary is often explicitly foregrounded in literary discourse. My study will focus on the semiotic preoccupations of Galdós's literature, which find expression both in the novels' vision of nineteenth-century Spanish society and in their reflection on their narrative and linguistic processes. By combining a general theoretical approach with the close analysis of five selected works, I hope to articulate the theory of the sign that is embodied in Galdós's texts.

Realism and Self-Consciousness

Nineteenth-century realist literature has traditionally been evaluated according to its ability to produce a plausible connection between

---

one particular semiological system" (Saussure, *Course in General Linguistics*, 68). Saussure's linguistic theory is contained in *Course in General Linguistics*, sets of lecture notes that his students published after his death. For a concise summary of Charles S. Peirce's complex semiotic system, see "Logic as Semiotic: The Theory of Signs." The various relationships (and contradictions) that theorists have noted between Saussure's "semiology" and Peirce's "semiotics" will not be discussed here, since they are not directly relevant to my study, which will focus on the analysis of specific texts.

7. *A Theory of Semiotics*, 6.

8. Jonathan Culler explores the nature of the literary text as a "second-order" semiotic system governed both by linguistic conventions and by special literary codes (*Ferdinand de Saussure*, 120–21).

9. Emile Benveniste, "The Semiology of Language." I elaborate upon this point in my discussion of the *Episodios nacionales* in Chapter 5.

the text and the world that it purports to represent. Influential thinkers, from Auerbach to Lukács, have propagated the widely accepted view that the representation of socio-historical and existential reality constitutes the foundation of modern realist fiction.[10] Galdós himself, in his speech to the Royal Academy, sets the novel's goal to be the concrete representation of a contemporary social reality that is undergoing a constant process of transformation.[11] As Kay Engler shows, the notion of referentiality (or the referential use of language) has traditionally been the constant in the critical definitions of nineteenth-century realism.[12]

In recent years, a growing number of critics have turned their attention to the self-conscious (or metafictional) tendencies of the novel.[13] Many have even suggested that the novel is by definition a self-examining and self-critical genre. Yet metafiction has generally been regarded as fundamentally contrary to the project of realism, especially in the nineteenth-century tradition. Robert Alter, for example, sees this tradition as leading novelists away from "the exploration of fiction as artifice."[14] If there is any manipulation of "artifice" in the realist novel, he claims, it never actually calls into question the ontological status of the invented world. Robert Scholes likewise establishes an opposition between the artistic virtuosity of metafiction (or "fabulation") and what he considers to be the positivistic tendency of nineteenth-century realism.[15] Michael Boyd criticizes realist fiction for "[pretending] to be what it is not" and characterizes self-reflexivity as a mode of "antirealism" that exposes this pretension.[16] Yet another critic, Patricia Waugh, declares both that realist fiction suppresses the dialogic potential of the metafictional genre and that metafiction is a tendency inherent in all novels. For her, realism represents a univocal fictional mode with a "materialist, posi-

10. Rafael Bosch, for example, attempts to show the relevance of Lukács's theory to the works of Galdós ("Galdós y la teoría de la novela de Lukács").

11. *Ensayos de crítica literaria*, 173–82.

12. *The Structure of Realism: The Novelas Contemporáneas of Benito Pérez Galdós*, 1–24.

13. See the following works: Robert Alter, *Partial Magic: The Novel as a Self-Conscious Genre*; Michael Boyd, *The Reflexive Novel: Fiction as Critique*; Linda Hutcheon, *Narcissistic Narrative*; Robert Scholes, *Fabulation and Metafiction*; Patricia Waugh, *Metafiction: The Theory and Practice of Self-Conscious Fiction*; and, in the Hispanic context, Robert Spires, *Beyond the Metafictional Mode: Directions in the Modern Spanish Novel*.

14. *Partial Magic*, 102.

15. *Fabulation*, 8.

16. *The Reflexive Novel*, 18–19.

tivist and empiricist world-view" against which the more explicitly metafictional modernist works are reacting. Later in her analysis of frame-breaking techniques, she declares that the use of this device in nineteenth-century fiction merely reinforces the illusion of reality rather than exposing the ontological status of the fiction.[17]

The tendency of these scholars to oppose realism to self-reflexivity can be explained by the basic convention of the realist novel, which Culler characterizes as "the expectation that readers will, through their contact with the text, be able to recognize a world which it produces or to which it refers."[18] This same convention makes possible the "reality effect," which Barthes defines in semiotic terms as "the direct collusion of a referent and a signifier."[19] If the creation of a referential illusion depends upon the expulsion of the "signified," any self-reference to the linguistic structure of the narrative, many critics seem to think, is potentially subversive to the representational goal of realist fiction. Yet realist fiction is not exempt from an awareness of its own conventions, as the example of Galdós will show. His works consistently reveal the extent to which mimesis and metafiction, referentiality and self-referentiality, are mutually dependent. The metafictional tendency of Galdós's fiction, at the same time as it lays bare its own conventions and questions the ontological status of the "world" in the text, affirms the power of language to create the illusion that this world is real. Galdós's fiction thus mirrors itself in the act of generating a mimetic convention.

Self-Consciousness in the Novels of Galdós

In her discussion of the modes of metafictional self-consciousness, Linda Hutcheon makes a distinction between diegetically and linguistically self-aware texts: the former explore the nature of their own nar-

17. *Metafiction*, 6, 32. One senses an arbitrariness in Waugh's distinction between "frame-breaks" that reinforce the connection between the real and the fictional worlds and frame-breaks that expose the ontological distinctness of these two worlds. Any frame-breaking technique can awaken the reader's awareness of the fictional process.

18. *Structuralist Poetics*, 192.

19. *The Rustle of Language*, 147. Umberto Eco calls this phenomenon "the referential fallacy," which posits a false correspondence between the "content of a sign-function" and a "real state of things" in the world (*A Theory of Semiotics*, 58).

rative processes, whereas the latter reveal an awareness of their own linguistic constitution.[20] These two categories of self-consciousness are not mutually exclusive; in fact, more often than not, they exist simultaneously within a given text. Galdós's novels dramatize the tension between referentiality and self-referentiality through both their diegetic and linguistic processes. *El amigo Manso*, one of Galdós's most overtly self-conscious novels, constitutes not only an ironic vision of the social, cultural, and political institutions of nineteenth-century Madrid or a tale of one man's existential lesson, but also a commentary on the creative act. As Kronik demonstrates, the narrator's account of his own fictional birth and death in the first and final chapters of the novel calls attention to the fictionality of the story contained within this frame. Moreover, the "interior novel," which is also about the theme of creation, self-consciously duplicates the "story of fiction" told by the narrator in the outer frame.[21]

The constant play between mimesis and metafiction on the level of the text's narrative processes mirrors the protagonist's own struggle with the problems of language in the interior text. Manso, a krausist educator and a rationalist philosopher devoted to "la investigación de la verdad" (the investigation of truth), lives his life according to the system of thought that he has constructed.[22] His endeavor to educate Manolo

20. *Narcissistic Narrative*, 22–23.

21. Kronik, "*El amigo Manso* and the Game of Fictive Autonomy," 74. Gustavo Pérez Firmat also interprets *El amigo Manso* as a self-conscious commentary on the relationship between creator and creation. He presents Galdós's novel as an example of "narrative metafiction," a work whose metafictionality "depends on an allegorical rendering of characters and events" ("Metafiction Again," 33). Other critics, while exploring different thematic concerns, have also touched upon the theme of fiction and reality in *El amigo Manso*. Nancy Newton, for example, links Galdós's method of characterization (Manso's evolution from object- to subject-centeredness), which is reflected in the novel's framing technique, to the work's concern with the relativity of reality ("*El amigo Manso* and the Relativity of Reality"). Harriet Turner shows how the confusion of reality and fiction in *El amigo Manso* paradoxically serves to "clarify social and moral values" ("The Control of Confusion and Clarity in *El amigo Manso*," 47). Ricardo Gullón, comparing Galdós's novel to Unamuno's *Niebla*, interprets Manso's unreal quality primarily as a metaphor for the protagonist's existential condition. At the same time, Gullón does recognize Manso's status as "personaje de papel, ente inventado que no recata, sino proclama su condición artificial" (a paper character, an invented being who does not conceal, but proclaims his condition as artifice; *Técnicas de Galdós*, 61).

22. Benito Pérez Galdós, *Obras completas (Novelas)*, 1:1186. All subsequent refer-

Peña and to discover in Irene "la mujer perfecta, la mujer positiva, la mujer razón" (the perfect woman, the positive woman, the woman of reason; 1:1215) shows that he sees language as the means to an absolute truth. Irene is a veiled sign that the narrator seeks to decipher ("soy lo más torpe del mundo para leer tus signos" [I am the world's greatest dullard at reading your signs], he declares on one occasion), just as Manolo represents a sign to be recreated according to Manso's educational philosophy, which strives for harmony between one's "true" self and society (1:1258). The ideal "truth" that he originally seeks in these characters, however, exists only in his imagination, for society's signs are fundamentally deceptive. As his two creations evade his authority, Manso faces the failure of his language of reason. Irene turns out to be not the ideal "mujer razón" (woman of reason) that Manso had imagined, but a slave to society's codes, "tan conforme al tipo de la muchedumbre" (so much in conformity with the standard crowd; 1:1306). Manso's language of reason gives rise not to truth but to an invented reality. His disciple Manolo Peña, who seeks not the truth but social acceptance and mobility, learns to manipulate the deceptive language of society. The cultivation of his linguistic art culminates in his speech before an institution of charity: he captivates his audience with empty words, which correspond to no meaning whatsoever. Peña thus transforms himself into a false sign, as the metaphor of his mask ("máscara de hipócrita" ["hypocrite's mask"]) suggests, rather than turning out to be the authentic sign that his instructor had sought to create (1:1307). As he loses control over his creations, Manso, for his part, recognizes the futility of his effort to find an absolute truth behind the signs about him. His inability to attain the truth through language self-consciously mirrors the absence of a real referent behind the narrator's written text, an absence that is symbolized by Manso's own "death" in the final chapter of the novel.[23] Both Manso and his creatures are mere signs on the page, whose apparent correspondence to a true referent is illusory.

---

ences to Galdós's *Novelas Españolas Contemporáneas* will appear in the text within parentheses. I am indebted to Robert Russell's translation of *El amigo Manso* (*Our Friend Manso*), which I have borrowed and modified in order to arrive at my own translations of Galdós's text. The English translations of all other texts cited in the Introduction are my own.

23. Diane Urey shows how the ironic narrator of *El amigo Manso*, who "destroys our ability to identify a single voice of truth," serves as a commentary on the ironic nature of language (*Galdós and the Irony of Language*, 74).

El amigo Manso is only one among the many works of Galdós that pose paradigmatic questions about language. The meditation on the sign in these works often finds expression in a character's concrete struggle with the problems of language. Galdós's creations, who are highly aware of the web of signs that surrounds them, decipher these signs in order simultaneously to (re)create them. Among the many interpreters within Galdós's texts, it is often possible to identify a single figure whose changing semiotic consciousness gives shape to the narration as a whole. This character never exists in isolation but must constantly respond to other voices in the text. The evolution of his or her vision of the sign is closely linked to one or more of the recurring themes, such as education, madness, story-telling, and writing, all of which can be viewed in semiotic terms.

The character's struggle to come to grips with his or her semiotic world through the acts of interpretation and creation is built upon a tension between two opposing visions of the sign. According to the first, the sign corresponds naturally to a true referent behind it; hence, it has the capacity to represent the truth. (This is the mimetic or referential function of the sign.) The contrary view of language holds that any apparent connection between words and things, the sign and the referent, is arbitrary and, therefore, deceptive. According to this perspective, language can never capture an absolute truth because it has no reality beyond itself. (This is the autonomous or self-referential impulse of the sign.) The character's desire to attain truth through language, on the one hand, and his or her desire to free it from the world, on the other, are set in perpetual conflict. Interpretation, which, by definition, is the search for truth or meaning, becomes inseparable from the creative act, through which the interpreting subject strives to transcend the limits of language and to produce an alternate language that conforms to his or her own desires. The struggle of the character to reconcile these two theories of the sign mirrors the novelistic process itself, which seeks to create the illusion of reality at the same time as it reveals itself to be an autonomous fiction.

The trajectory of the character's interpretive activity, as well as the resolution of his or her struggle with the problems of language, remains unique to each of Galdós's novels. The chapters that follow will examine individually the various forms that this struggle takes in a number of representative texts chosen from among the *Novelas españolas contemporáneas* and the *Episodios nacionales*. The novels selected belong to different periods of Galdós's career as a writer: *La corte de Carlos IV* (1873) (in the context of the entire first series of the *Episodios*), *El doctor Centeno* (1883), *Fortunata y Jacinta* (1886–1887), *La incógnita* and *Realidad* (1889), and *Tristana* (1892). These novels represent a wide range of narrative forms and techniques, among which are the epistolary and dialogue forms, the third-person narration, and the first-person fictional autobiography. The narrative structure of these works, which determines the relationship between the narrator and the interpreter figure within the text (even in cases when the two are the same), is of central importance to the study of the semiotic process. In Galdós's third-person narrations, the narrator often simultaneously participates in and offers an ironic perspective on the character's struggle with the sign. In the first-person narration, the evolution of the protagonist's semiotic consciousness is revealed in the distance between the narrating subject and the narrated self. The epistolary novel, in which the distance between these two selves is minimal, explicitly foregrounds the character's interpretive activity. The dialogue form allows each character but one voice that is in perpetual conflict with the others.

Seeking to define the implicit theory of language that these texts dramatize, this study will make no attempt to impose a diachronic reading on them.[24] Instead, I have chosen to organize the discussion of Galdós's novels on the basis of paradigmatic considerations. The use of paradigms, however, is not intended to reduce the complexity of the individual text to predetermined or categorical patterns, but simply to provide a useful framework for the analyses that follow. The first chapter serves an umbrella function for the subsequent chapters. The undecidability between two contradictory visions of the sign, which defines Maximiliano Rubín's "madness" in *Fortunata y Jacinta*, represents the basic paradigm that underlies all of the novels under discussion. In *El doctor Centeno* (Chapter 2), the principal interpreter figure struggles to overcome the two opposing impulses of the sign by creating the myth of the natural sign. Although this myth is ultimately subverted, it domi-

---

24. The task of criticism, as Jonathan Culler suggests, is to approximate the "poetics" of the text itself, to read the work as the "vehicle of an implicit theory of language or of other semiotic systems" (*Structuralist Poetics*, 98). See also his foreword to Todorov's *The Poetics of Prose*, in which he comments on the fusion between poetics and criticism in the latter's readings of literary works. For Culler, Todorov's criticism, which "becomes an investigation of how a particular work resists, complies with, and implicitly comments upon the general signifying practices of literary discourse" (12), is guided and informed by poetics.

nates a greater part of the character's trajectory in the novel. The protagonist of *Tristana* (Chapter 3), in contrast, strives to beget a completely new language that has no connection to a referent. Her desire is to fabricate autonomous signs rather than natural ones. The novels treated in Chapters 2 and 3 can thus be seen as diametrically opposed: the semiotic activity of their respective protagonists is projected toward antithetical ends. In *La incógnita*, the basic paradigm presented in *Fortunata y Jacinta* is explicitly foregrounded through the narrator's writing. The epistolary novel is distinct from the other three works in that the narrator himself is the principal interpreter figure. Finally, the fifth chapter on the first series of the *Episodios nacionales* has been included to show that Galdós's "historical novels" are no less self-reflexive about their linguistic processes than are his *Novelas españolas contemporáneas*. The contradictory roles of the narrator-protagonist as historian, on the one hand, and as creator of fictions, on the other, are yet a further manifestation of the semiotic conflict that the four *Novelas españolas contemporáneas* dramatize.

In its synchronic orientation, this study will depart from the chronological readings of such prominent scholars as Casalduero, Correa, and Montesinos. Given the quantity of Galdós's literary production and the complexity of each of his novels, any generalization about the evolution of his thematic or linguistic concerns runs the risk of oversimplification. Moreover, linguistic self-awareness, the subject of this study, remains a constant throughout all of Galdós's literary production, from the *Novelas de la primera época* to the later series of the *Episodios nacionales*. Even Galdós's earliest novels reveal a preoccupation with the problems of language. *La sombra* (1870), for example, dramatizes the interpretive act of an unnamed character-narrator, who seeks to reconstruct the truth behind the strange tale of his friend Don Anselmo. The narrator, who at first questions the truth of Anselmo's narration, gradually suspends his disbelief until he comes to treat the events of his friend's account as if they had really occurred. By the end of the novel, the narrator's own sense of reality has become transformed to the extent that he asks himself whether the fictional Paris had indeed reappeared on Anselmo's canvas. His initially skeptical attitude toward the sign thus gives way to a belief in the direct correspondence between language and reality. His transcription of Anselmo's narration self-consciously reflects the transformation of his own vision of language. In *Doña Perfecta* (1876), another novel of the *Primera época*, the protagonist's struggle against the provincialism of Orbajosa can be interpreted in linguistic terms. Pepe Rey's love of truth, reflected in his faith in science, is set in conflict with the falseness of a provincial society whose signs never correspond to the reality that they suggest. Rey himself notes the disjunction between words and the reality behind them: "Palabras hermosas, realidad prosaica y miserable" (Beautiful words, prosaic and miserable reality), he says. "Aquí todo es al revés. La ironía no cesa" (Here everything is backwards. The irony is never-ending; 1:417–18). *Orbajosa* itself is a polysemic word that signifies two contradictory realities: the vulgar *orb ajosa* (garlicky world) and the glorious *urbs augusta* (august city). *Doña Perfecta* illustrates the struggle between Pepe Rey's language of reason and the false language through which the *orbajosenses* have created a world of illusion. In the end, both Pepe Rey's "reason" and the "glorious Spain" of the *orbajosenses* are exposed as false constructs of language. The novel therefore deconstructs the very notion of an absolute truth.

In the existing synchronic studies of Galdós, most notably those of Ricardo Gullón and Kay Engler, the analysis of the structural and stylistic elements of Galdós's novels seems to become an end in itself, rather than the vehicle for a more global theory of language behind these works.[25] Only Diane Urey, in her discussion of irony, considers the technical aspects of the *Novelas españolas contemporáneas* (characterization, setting, and position of the narrator) to reflect the nature of language. Her deconstruction of "representational meaning" in Galdós's opus, however, tends to overlook the nature of the text as a semiotic *process* that dramatizes the perpetual play between referentiality and autonomy, presence and absence, meaning and the infinite deferral of the signified.[26]

My own critical position implies a particular role for the reader. Since the absence of a single voice behind Galdós's texts makes the recovery of an original meaning—whether it is historical truth, an existential essence, or an ideological message—an impossible goal for the

---

25. Ricardo Gullón explores the workings of Galdós's imaginary world through an analysis of the techniques and structure of four novels, from *Doña Perfecta* to *Fortunata y Jacinta* (*Técnicas de Galdós*). Engler, along a similar line, sets out to define realism's "formula of art" structurally by examining the "patterns of relationships between the narrator and his narration" in Galdós's *Novelas españolas contemporáneas* (*The Structure of Realism*, 17). Engler's analysis of narrative structure in the individual works is illuminating; however, her rather vague conclusion that "comprehensiveness and coherence characterize Galdós' realism" suggests the absence of a coherent theoretical explanation for her observations (187).

26. *Galdós and the Irony of Language*, 125.

reader, he or she must construct his or her own interpretation. As Barthes has said in "The Death of the Author": "In the multiplicity of writing, everything is to be *disentangled*, nothing *deciphered*."[27] The role of the reader is to "disentangle" the various strands of potential meaning in the texts and to weave them into his or her own text. At the same time, he or she cannot construct meanings without positing some notion of a structure that is implicit in the texts. All acts of interpretation involve a dynamic interaction between these structures and the conventions that the reader brings to the texts.[28] As a twentieth-century reader influenced by recent tendencies in fiction and in theory, I am privileging a vision of the literary work as a sustained meditation on language. Although what I call "semiotic consciousness" cannot be seen strictly as an inherent attribute that resides within the texts, the concept can provide a useful interpretive framework for the critic. Moreover, this framework contains within itself a self-critique, since it dramatizes the undecidability between two different ways of interpreting the text. In the analyses that follow, I hope to show the complexity of Galdós's realist enterprise, which is inseparable from his works' self-conscious reflection on language.

27. *Image-Music-Text*, 147.

28. See Wolfgang Iser, who explores the space in which this interaction between the reader and the text occurs (*The Act of Reading*). Although Iser views reading as a process of creation, he nevertheless posits the existence of certain textual structures or "signals" that are to be actualized by the reader. The process by which the reader, according to Iser, constantly formulates and modifies the signified through his or her interaction with the text is also built upon the tension between interpretation and creation, between the presence and the absence of meaning.

1

Maxi and the Signs of Madness

Reading as Creation in *Fortunata y Jacinta*

> Though this be madness, yet there is method in't.
>
> —Shakespeare, *Hamlet*

At the beginning of Part 2 of *Fortunata y Jacinta*, Maximiliano Rubín, in a confused state between sleep and wakefulness, reflects upon the arbitrariness of the linguistic sign:

Verdaderamente—decía él—, ¿por qué ha de ser una cosa más real que la otra? ¿Por qué no ha de ser sueño lo del día y vida efectiva lo de la noche? Es cuestión de nombres y de que diéramos en llamar *dormir* a lo que llamamos *despertar*, y *acostarse* al *levantarse*... ¿Qué razones hay para que no diga yo ahora, mientras me visto: "Maximiliano, ahora te estás echando a dormir. Vas a pasar mala noche con pesadilla y todo, o sea con clase de *Materia farmacéutica animal*..."? (2:597)

(Actually—he said to himself—why should one thing be more real than another? Why shouldn't daytime events be a dream and what happens at night be real life? It's a question of names, of our taking it upon ourselves to call *sleeping* what we call *waking*, and *going to bed*, *getting up*... What reason prevents me from saying, as I'm getting dressed: "Maximiliano, now you're getting ready to go to sleep. You're going to have a bad night with a nightmare and everything, I mean, a class on 'Animal Matter in Pharmaceutics'..."?)[1]

This moment of semiotic disjunction marks the beginning of Max-imiliano's supposed madness, which defines his function in the novel as

---

1. I have based my translations of *Fortunata y Jacinta* on Agnés Gullón's work, with slight modifications of my own. All other translations henceforward are my own.

an interpreter of signs and creator of fictions.[2] Maxi questions the established relationship between words and things, signs and their referents. These words (*dormir* and *despertar*, *acostarse* and *levantarse* [*sleeping and waking up, going to bed* and *getting up*]), he declares, are nothing more than names, whose correspondence to the reality behind them (*despertar* to *vida efectiva* [real life] and *dormir* to *sueño* [dream]) is arbitrary: the rest of society fails to understand that signs only signify through conventions.[3] Significantly, Maxi's reflection on language marks the first moment in which the narrator of the novel allows the reader to enter directly into the character's thoughts.

The traditional approach to Maxi's deviation from society has been to treat him as a subject for a psychological case study.[4] This methodology, however valid from a psychiatrist's perspective, is limiting for the literary critic, who must maintain a critical distance from the text: to treat a fictional character as if he or she were a real person is to lose awareness of the fact that the text is ultimately composed of signs.[5] As

2. Similarly, in her reading of Balzac's "The Illustrious Gaudissart" as a "dramatized meditation on language," Shoshana Felman characterizes the madman's discourse as the postulation of a "discontinuity between sign and signified" (*Writing and Madness*, 104, 108).

3. Maxi's questioning of language anticipates the fundamental principle of Saussurean linguistics: the arbitrariness of the sign. For Saussure's theory, see his *Course in General Linguistics*, especially Part 1 (65–100).

4. See Angel Garma, "Jaqueca, seudo-oligofrenia y delirio en un personaje de Pérez Galdós"; E. D. Randolph, "A Source for Maxi Rubín in *Fortunata y Jacinta*"; Geoffrey Ribbans, *Fortunata y Jacinta*; J. C. Ullman and G. H. Allison, "Galdós as Psychiatrist in *Fortunata y Jacinta*." Arthur Holmberg, who interprets Maxi's "madness" from a different angle, perceives in the character's "schizophrenia" the embodiment of a tension between two opposing literary tendencies—romanticism and naturalism—that Galdós seeks to reconcile in the work ("Louis Lambert and Maximiliano Rubín: The Inner Vision and the Outer Man"). Joaquín Casalduero similarly sees Maxi as an incarnation of the conflict between "la Materia y el Espíritu" (Matter and Spirit; *Vida y obra de Galdós*, 90). This view is not incompatible with my own; however, these critics neglect the specifically *linguistic* nature of Maxi's "madness." From yet another viewpoint, Stephen Gilman considers Maxi as a failed existential hero who, unlike Fortunata, becomes increasingly alienated from his "inner consciousness": "The latter [Maxi], who begins with an exalted sense of the interior space of his consciousness, seems to us ever more diminished as we go on reading. Not only do his illusions about himself and others cut him off from experience, but he actually seems to grow backwards. By the end he has shrunken himself to a purely rational autonomy, encaged in a mind as self-sufficiently sick as Fortunata's is healthy" (*Galdós and the Art of the European Novel*, 339).

5. Another example of such loss of distance is José Montesinos's commentary on

Roland Barthes repeatedly claims in his *Critical Essays*, the essential reality of literature lies not in any concealed signified but in language itself, a conventional system of signs. From this perspective, the process by which human beings fabricate meaning acquires new importance as a subject of literary studies. Maximiliano Rubín exemplifies Barthes's *homo significans*, who is constantly making sense of the signs of the world around him.[6]

Maxi's "madness" can be interpreted as a semiotic struggle that self-consciously mirrors the process of the novel itself.[7] The changing vision of the sign that underlies his interpretive activity represents the tension in the text between mimesis and fictional autonomy, referentiality and self-referentiality. In one of his famous essays, Barthes defines the need for a "new" object, the Text, which eliminates the traditional separation between reading and writing by "joining them in a single signifying practice."[8] Linda Hutcheon similarly asserts that one of the fundamental characteristics of modern metafiction is the near equation of the acts of reading and writing.[9] *Fortunata y Jacinta* exhibits its "modernity" as metafiction by explicitly dramatizing the inseparability of these two acts through the interpretive activity of a character *within the text*. As Naomi Schor states: "Novels are not only about speaking and writing (*encoding*), but also about reading, and by reading I mean the *decoding* of all manner of signs and signals."[10] The signs within the text tell the reader about the text itself as a sign. In the case of *Fortunata y Jacinta*, Maxi's interpretation and creation of signs call attention to the semiotic process of

---

Fortunata y Jacinta. At the same time as he declares, "Rubín no es meramente una historia clínica" (Rubín is not merely a clinical case), he treats the character as a live subject for a psychological study. Montesinos says that Maxi "es tan de carne y hueso como pueda serlo Fortunata" (is as much flesh and blood as Fortunata could be), as if Fortunata herself were other than a fictional being (*Galdós*, 263).

6. *Critical Essays*, 213–20.

7. John W. Kronik, in his "Galdosian Reflections," demonstrates that *Fortunata y Jacinta* is a self-conscious reflection upon artistic creation. He reads the fourth chapter of Part 3, "Un curso de filosofía práctica" (A course in practical philosophy), as a fiction-within-a-fiction that dramatizes this process through Feijoo's "fabrication" of Fortunata.

8. *Image-Music-Text*, 162.

9. *Narcissistic Narrative*, 27. Hutcheon defines metafiction as "fiction about fiction—that is, fiction that includes within itself a commentary on its own narrative and/or linguistic identity" (ibid., 1).

10. "Fiction as Interpretation/Interpretation as Fiction," 168.

the novel and, by doing so, invite a reading of the text as an implicit theory of language.[11]

Many of the other characters in *Fortunata y Jacinta,* as well as the narrator, also struggle to come to terms with the signs that form their world. An important semiotic system is society itself, whose signs never mean what they seem to say. Fortunata's thoughts summarize this constantly recurring theme of the novel: "¡Qué cosas hay, pero qué cosas!... Un mundo que se ve, y otro que está debajo, escondido..." (What things you find, what things!... There's the world you see and then there's another one, hidden underneath... ; 2:799). Society's hypocrisy—the gap between outer appearance and reality—can be seen, in semiotic terms, as a disjunction between the sign and the referent. An entire series of characters—Doña Lupe, Nicolás Rubín, and Evaristo Feijoo, among others—rely on their awareness of society's codes in their efforts to "redeem" Fortunata through instruction. Her education, as education always must, represents an attempt to initiate the individual into the semiotic system of society. The characters of the novel are not only aware of social signs; oftentimes they are also conscious of the signs of specifically linguistic constructs within the text. Jacinta, for example, must constantly decipher Juanito Santa Cruz's "narrations" for signs of truth.[12] The narrator of the novel himself, during moments when he steps out of his role of omniscience, engages in the act of interpretation in order to arrive at the truth behind the events that he narrates. At one point, for example, he tries to decipher Jacinta in the act of interpreting Juanito Santa Cruz's story, as he asks himself: "¿Creía Jacinta aquellas cosas, o aparentaba creerlas como Sancho las bolas que D. Quixote le contó de la cueva de Montesinos?" (Did Jacinta believe those things, or was she pretending to believe them, like Sancho when Don Quixote fed him hoaxes about the cave of Montesinos?; 2:750).[13]

Of all the interpreters within the novel, Maximiliano Rubín maintains the greatest consciousness of the signs around him; consequently

---

11. Jonathan Culler, in a chapter entitled "Linguistic Metaphors in Criticism," discusses the tendency in modern criticism to treat the literary text as "an investigation of language itself" (*Structuralist Poetics,* 105–6).

12. John W. Kronik stresses the importance of various characters' "interior narrations" within the novel for the narrative project of the work as a whole. See "Narraciones interiores en *Fortunata y Jacinta.*"

13. The use of the *mise en abyme* technique allows the reader to become more conscious of his or her own interpretive role: here, the reader is interpreting the narrator's interpretation of Jacinta's interpretation of Juanito's story. For a discussion of this literary device, see Hutcheon, *Narcissistic Narrative,* 53–56.

he is better able to manipulate them in order to fabricate fictions. What other characters (and critics alike) perceive as Maxi's madness is, paradoxically, based on a highly sophisticated awareness of the problems of language. Although he does not appear until Part 2 of the novel and disappears as an explicit presence through most of Part 3, he traces a coherent trajectory as a self-aware reader and creator of signs. Furthermore, it is his voice that closes the novel with a statement on the paradox of fiction and of language.

With his attempted subversion of the conventions of signification, seen in his early-morning meditation on the sign, Maxi engages the possibility of freeing himself from a reality that fails to correspond to his desires.[14] Desire always exists as an empty sign. For Maxi, language represents the means of filling the absence behind the sign with the illusion of presence: "el goce de Maximiliano consistía en pensar e imaginar libremente y a sus anchas, figurándose realidades y volando sin tropiezo por los espacios de lo posible, aunque fuera improbable" (Maximiliano's pleasure consisted of thinking and musing at his own free will, imagining realities and flying straight through the space of what was possible, although improbable; 2:597). According to René Girard's theory, the subject does not desire spontaneously but always in imitation of another.[15] In *Fortunata y Jacinta*, society mediates and defines Maxi's desire at the same time as it marginalizes him. Introduced to the reader as "raquítico, de naturaleza pobre y linfática, absolutamente privado de gracias personales" (rickety, weak, lymphatic, and completely devoid of physical charm; 2:592), he constantly constructs fictions in order to bridge the gap between himself and the society with which he is at odds.

Maxi's desire for a "mujer honrada" (decent woman)—a construct of society's codes—precedes his love for any specific woman.[16] Before he

14. Rodríguez-Puértolas, who cites this same passage, views Maxi's desire for freedom in completely negative terms: as an attempt to escape not from society, but from "Nature." Maxi's "madness," according to Puértolas, is a consequence of the typically bourgeois infraction of the laws of "Nature" (*Galdós: burguesía y revolución*, 61–92). Curiously, Eduardo Urbina takes exactly the opposite view by considering the transcendence of Maxi and of other "redeemers" in the novel as "un intento de reconciliar creativamente naturaleza y sociedad" (an attempt to reconcile nature and society creatively) ("Mesías y redentores: constante estructural y motivo temático en *Fortunata y Jacinta*," 380).

15. *Deceit, Desire and the Novel*, 1–52.

16. For lack of an exact English equivalent for the culturally charged Spanish word *honrada*, I follow Agnes Gullón's example and translate it as "decent." Given

meets Fortunata for the first time, he pursues anonymous women through
the streets of Madrid in an attempt to read their appearance for signs of
honradez. Soon he masters the social sign, which produces a correspondence between external appearance and the condition of honor, or
decency: "Pronto supo distinguir de *clases,* es decir, llegó a tener tan
buen ojo, que conocía al instante las que eran honradas y las que no"
(Soon he learned to distinguish women by their *class*; that is to say, he
developed such a keen eye that he could tell in a flash which ones were
decent and which ones were not; 2:597). Maxi's search for a reality (true
honradez) behind the sign (the outward "appearance" of the women) is
senseless, given that he is at odds with the codes of society. At the same
time, as is evident in his obsession with the idea of *honradez,* he is unable
to free himself from social language. Even his initial questioning of
signs represents an inversion of conventions rather than an absolute
freedom from them. Instead of suggesting a completely arbitrary system of language to replace the existing conventions, he simply reverses
the relationship between the signifier (*dormir* and *despertar, acostarse* and
levantarse) and the signified (the concepts of *sueño* and *vida efectiva*). From
the first moment in which he questions these conventions, Maxi becomes caught in the conflict between the language of society and that of
his own fictions. As reader of signs, he is more aware of this constant
tension than any other character in the novel.

When he fortuitously finds a woman who, he believes, embodies all
of his desires, Maxi seeks to recreate her according to his knowledge of
the social code of *honradez.* Fortunata, a "natural" woman of the *pueblo,*
unrefined and uneducated, becomes the perfect object of his creative
enterprise.[17] As he transforms her into an ideal ("Dos Fortunatas
existían entonces: una, la de carne y hueso; otra, la que Maximiliano

the patriarchal nature of the Spanish honor code, the woman's honor is defined not in
terms of absolute moral qualities that she possesses, but rather by the *appearance* of
social decency as defined by man: she is no more than a *sign* of man's honor.

17. Maxi's attitude toward Fortunata conforms to the traditional (and, many would
say, patriarchal) notion of woman as nature and man as culture. The French feminist Hélène Cixous, for example, links this opposition (female/male, nature/cul-
ture) to the privileging of speech over writing, logocentrism over "open-ended textuality" (Toril Moi, *Sexual/Textual Politics: Feminist Literary Theory,* 108). The position
of the implied author, however, cannot necessarily be identified with that of the male
character, as Galdós's novels often deconstruct all such hierarchical oppositions.
Consequently, I have chosen to focus on the dynamics of creator-creation, author-
text, rather than on the possible political implications behind these relationships.

llevaba en su mente" [Two Fortunatas existed during this period: the one of flesh and blood, and another one that Maximiliano carried around in his mind; 2:607]), Maxi awakens to a consciousness of the insufficiency of language, which is unable to mediate the distance between the real and the ideal:

> Tratando de medir el cariño que sentía por su amiga, Maximiliano hallaba pálida e inexpresiva la palabra *querer*, teniendo que recurrir a las novelas y a la poesía en busca del verbo *amar*, tan usado en los ejercicios gramaticales como olvidado en el lenguaje corriente. Y aun aquel verbo le parecía desabrido para expresar la dulzura y ardor de su cariño. Adorar, idolatrar y otros cumplían mejor su oficio de dar a conocer la pasión exaltada de un joven enclenque de cuerpo y robusto de espíritu. (2:607)

> (In his attempts to measure the affection that he felt for his friend, Maximiliano found the word *querer* [to love] pale and inexpressive, and he had to resort to novels and poetry in order to find the verb *amar*, which is as common in grammatical drills as it is forgotten in everyday language. And even that verb seemed to him too stale to express the tenderness and ardor of his affection. *Adore* and *idolize* and other such words were better at helping the weak-bodied, high-spirited youth declare his exalted passion.)

Maxi's search for words forms part of the creative process through which he transfigures his beloved into an ideal. Significantly, it is in literature that he seeks the appropriate language for the expression of his sentiments. Fiction represents the realm of self-sufficient signs that need not seek a referent in reality.[18] Maxi's fabrication of Fortunata through language reflects the process by which all literature seeks to create an illusion of presence through words.

His creative enterprise, significantly, corresponds to his linguistic transformation. Maxi gradually gains command over the word after he

---

18. In a slightly different context, Germán Gullón asserts: "el lector debe entender que el autor no sólo estaba creando un mundo ficticio, sino haciéndolo autónomo y autorreferencial" (the reader should understand that the author was not only creating a fictional world, but also making it autonomous and self-referential) (*La novela como acto imaginativo*, 120–21). Gullón's statement is also relevant to the fictions of Maxi and of other characters in the text.

establishes relations with Fortunata. At first, he is unable to defend himself verbally against Doña Lupe's objection to his courtship with Fortunata. The narrator speaks of Maxi as he confronts his aunt's disapproval: "pensó en defenderse; pero no podía encontrar las armas, es decir, las palabras" (he thought of defending himself, but he couldn't find the weapons, that is, the words; 2:628). Soon afterwards, however, he learns to manipulate words with relative facility. After hearing her nephew defend his love for Fortunata with great eloquence, Doña Lupe exclaims with surprise: "No me engatusarás con palabritas. Vaya, que de la noche a la mañana has aprendido unos términos y unos floreos de frases que me tienen pasmada... Estás hecho un poeta... en toda la extensión de la palabra" (You won't wheedle me with pretty words. Well now, overnight you've picked up fancy terms and phrases that leave me stunned... You're a regular poet... in the full sense of the word; 2:635).[19]

Maxi idealizes Fortunata not as a Dulcinea del Toboso, but as a "burguesa honrada" (decent bourgeois).[20] As her social and moral "redeemer," he seeks to correct her "incultura rasa" (utter lack of culture) by teaching her the language of the bourgeoisie, that is, to "adquirir ciertas ideas y aprender palabras finas y decentes" (acquire certain notions and learn refined, decent words; 2:607). He invents the idea of the "dos honradeces" (two kinds of decency): by creating the social appearance of *honradez*, Maxi believes that he can somehow produce a true "honradez del alma" (decency of the soul; 2:599) in Fortunata. His efforts to construct a sign that corresponds to a desired referent are subverted by the reappearance of Juanito Santa Cruz at the end of Part 2. Despite Maxi's failure to mold Fortunata completely according to the conventions of society, she has gained, in the process of her "education," a certain consciousness of the language of the bourgeoisie. By the time Maxi proposes marriage to her, she has already internalized to some degree the bourgeois conception of *honradez* as the appearance of social status and propriety: "Pero ¡calcula tú, mujer," she exclaims to herself,

19. Yet another event, Maxi's substitution of the *hucha* (piggy-bank), which immediately follows his first encounter with Fortunata, anticipates his subsequent mastery of the sign. After destroying his bank in order to remove the coins that are inside, he substitutes it with another one of equal size and shape in order to conceal this act from his aunt's knowledge. His ability to create a deceptive sign marks his incipient semiotic consciousness.

20. Maxi's artistic enterprise is similar to that of Feijoo, who later in Part 3 tries to recreate Fortunata according to the codes of society (Kronik, "Galdosian Reflections," 290–310).

"ser honrada, ser casada, señora de tal... persona decente!..." (But just think, woman... to be decent, married, Mrs. somebody... a decent person!... ; 2:614). At the beginning of Part 3, when Juanito abandons her for the second time, Fortunata, in a state of distress, affirms her *honradez*, which she interprets to mean fidelity. In her (relative) linguistic innocence, she appropriates a code of bourgeois society into her own language, but without fully internalizing this society's system of signs.

The frustration of Maxi's attempt to possess Fortunata through his mission of reform leads him to seek refuge in spiritualist philosophy. Challenging the materialist world view of those who frequent the café, he declares to his brother Juan Pablo: "Pues a eso que tú llamas fuerza yo lo llamo espíritu, el Verbo, el querer universal, y volvemos a la misma historia, al Dios uno y creador y al alma que de Él emana" (What you call force, I call "soul," the Word, universal love; and we come back to the same old story—to God as creator and unity and to the soul that emanates from Him; 2:782). Maxi's philosophy, based partly on the New Testament and partly on idealist thought, has at its center the idea of the Word (*el Verbo*), which brings together the semiotic systems of religion (Christianity) and of language.[21] The Word, which is incarnated in Christ according to the Gospel of John, also maintains its literal meaning as language, or *logos*. "El querer universal," by which Maxi refers to spiritual love on one level, also has the connotation of "want," or "desire."[22] The Word, in both the theological and linguistic sense, forms the basis of his new fiction.

Maxi's fictional theology finds expression in a vision in which an angel reveals to him that if Fortunata is pregnant, it is "por obra del *Pensamiento puro*" (the work of *Pure thought*; 2:850). According to Maxi, this vision occurs to him in one of his dreams. (In this dream, he consumes a bottle of morphine and falls into a deep lethargy, at which time the angel appears at his side.) Not only does his dream, like those of many other Galdosian characters, represent the creative process, but its status as a dream within yet another dream calls attention to the

21. See Kenneth Burke, who interprets theology as "logology": "words about God" as "words about words" (*The Rhetoric of Religion*, 1).

22. Language represents the desire for the signified because it is predicated on an absence. Language thus perpetuates desire, which, in turn, leads to the creation of language. Elaine Haddad examines Maxi's new "spiritualism" as a sublimation of his desires, but without noting the complexity of the relationship between language/fiction and desire ("Maximiliano Rubín," 108).

distance that separates the character from reality.[23] His new fiction constitutes a rewriting of the New Testament, in which Fortunata becomes transformed into the Virgin, and her illegitimate child into the Messiah. Maxi identifies himself with Joseph, the figure of the absent father. The redemptive mission of the Messiah symbolizes for Maxi the idealist state of *Pensamiento puro* (*Pure thought*) to which he aspires, in which the soul is freed from the flesh, the individual from society, and, by extension, language from the world. His recreation of Fortunata is no longer based on the codes of bourgeois society, but on the language of a larger fiction that he invents by combining Christianity and idealism.

The ideal of *Pensamiento puro* that Maximiliano Rubín claims to have achieved marks the height of his madness from the viewpoint of society. In order to explain this state to Doña Lupe, Maxi makes use of the pharmaceutical metaphor of the *panacea*:

—No es mal nombre [panacea] si usted se lo quiere dar—dijo el pobre chico, exaltándose más a cada palabra—. De *pan*, que significa todo... , y *akos*, que es lo mismo que decir *remedio*. Que lo sana y purifica todo, vamos... (2:864)

"That's not a bad name, if that's what you want to call it," said the poor boy, more exalted with each word. "From *pan*, which means everything... , and *akos*, which is the same as saying *remedy*. It heals and purifies everything, it's..."

With his etymological consciousness, he converts Doña Lupe's literal

---

23. In *Miau*, a similar experience befalls Luisito Cadalso, whose visions of God gradually take over reality and ultimately determine the fate of his grandfather, the *cesante* Ramón de Villaamil. After Luisito suffers a temporary inability to evoke the figure of God, the child dreams that he sees God's apparition: "Lo doloroso para Cadalsito era que soñaba que la veía, lo que no era lo mismo que verla. Al menos no estaba satisfecho, y su mente forcejeaba en un razonar muy penoso y absurdo, diciendo: 'No es éste, no es éste... , porque yo no le veo, sino sueño que le veo y no me habla, sino sueño que me habla'" (The painful thing for Cadalsito was that he dreamed that he saw it, which was not the same as actually seeing it. He wasn't satisfied, at least, and his mind struggled in a very arduous and absurd reasoning, saying: "No, this isn't it, this isn't it... , because I don't see him, but rather I dream that I see him and he doesn't speak to me: I dream that he speaks to me"; 2:1057). By self-consciously scrutinizing his dream-within-a-dream, Luisito calls attention to the process by which he fabricates a world of the imagination.

idea of *panacea* as a cure-all drug into a metaphor for his philosophical system. This state of purification constitutes the absolute negation of the flesh ("la bestia carcelera" [the imprisoning beast]), of society (with its materialist principles), and of the link between words and things: it is the culmination of the process that he summarizes as "liberación por el desprendimiento, por la anulación" (liberation through detachment, through annulment; 2:902). This goal, which he proposes for himself and for Fortunata, however, is impossible as long as human beings remain enslaved to society's codes. The only way to achieve complete freedom from these codes is through death, through a collective suicide. Maxi, who begins Fortunata's recreation by manipulating her, a sign, from within society's system of signs, now seeks to liberate her completely from these codes by putting an end to her life. Yet, as long as the object of his desire ties him to society, he is unable to realize his suicidal plan.

Maximiliano Rubín's semiotic project takes yet another turn after Fortunata leaves him for the last time to give birth to her illegitimate son. After his wife's disappearance, he returns to socially defined reason by completely renouncing his spiritualist philosophy. In a conversation with Juan Pablo, Maxi acknowledges that his envisioning of Fortunata's son as the new Messiah has been a product of his imagination. Whether he truly believed in his previous philosophy at one time is secondary to his recognition of its fictional nature. He is aware that jealousy, inseparable from desire, lies at the root of his fiction: "Lo que hay es que me había entrado en aquellos días una idea de lo más estrafalario que te puedes imaginar, una idea que debía de ser criada aquí, en el seno cerebral, donde fermenta eso que llaman celos" (What happened is that during those days an idea got into my head, the most outrageous idea that you can possibly imagine, an idea that must have grown here, in the recess of the brain where what they call jealousy ferments; 2:913). Jealousy represents the subversion of the sign of love that he tries to read in Fortunata: it results from his inability to link the appearance of *honradez* to matrimonial fidelity itself. Later, in an attempt to console his friend José Ido del Sagrario, another madman in society's view, Maxi asserts his present state of "sanity" in opposition to his past state of "madness": "durante una temporada he estado como usted... , muchí - simo peor. Yo inventaba religiones; yo quería que todo el género humano se matara; yo esperaba el Mesías... Pues aquí me tiene tan sano y tan bueno" (For a while I was like you... , but much worse. I invented religions; I wanted all humanity to be killed off; I was waiting for the

Messiah… And here I am, all sane and well again; 2:925).[24] In renouncing his previous fiction, Maxi adopts society's vision of sanity as
conformity to its codes. His return to socially defined sanity, therefore,
appropriately corresponds to his defense of the logic of society. His
renunciation of mystical philosophy and his supposed reintegration
into society result in his conversion to "reason."

The narrator of the novel ironically adopts society's point of view and
acclaims Maxi's newly gained reason:

Una diferencia había entre la deambulación pasada y la presente. Aquélla era nocturna y tenía algo de sonambulismo o de ideación enfermiza;
ésta era diurna, y a causa de las buenas condiciones del ambiente solar
en que se producía, resultaba más sana y más conforme con la higiene
cerebroespinal. En aquélla, la mente trabajaba en la ilusión, fabricando
mundos vanos con la espuma que echan de sí las ideas bien batidas; en
ésta trabajaba en la razón, entreteniéndose en ejercicios de lógica, sen-
tando principios y obteniendo consecuencias con admirable facilidad.
(2:919)

(There was one difference between his earlier meandering and the present one. The former took place at night and resembled sleepwalking or
sickly ideation; the latter took place during the day, and due to the
favorable conditions of the solar atmosphere in which it was produced, it
was healthier and more conducive to cerebrospinal hygiene. In the former, his mind worked in the realm of illusion, fabricating insubstantial
worlds out of the foam spewed up by well-beaten ideas; in the latter, it

24. José Ido del Sagrario can be seen as Maxi's double: his "madness," like that
of Maxi, is inseparable from his creative activity. His fits of jealousy, one of the
manifestations of his "madness," have their root in literature. Having been a writer
of popular novels, Ido loses distance from the world of his own creation: "todo to-
cante a damas infieles, guapetonas, que se iban de picos pardos con unos duques
muy adúlteros… , y los maridos trinando…" (all about unfaithful ladies, real attrac-
tive ones, who'd go off on the sly with adulterous dukes… and the husbands fum-
ing… ; 2:548). His "novela *Pitusiana*," through which he later awakens Jacinta's
imagination, is also based on the conventions of the *folletín*. As Juanito Santa Cruz
must remind her regarding this fiction, "si como historia el caso es falso, como novela
es cursi" (if as a story the events are false, as a novel it's tasteless; 2:580). For a
discussion of Ido del Sagrario as Galdós's alter ego, see Rodríguez, "Ido del Sagrario: notas sobre el otro novelista en Galdós."

worked in the realm of reason, dallying in logical exercises, asserting principles, and obtaining consequences with admirable ease.)

This passage employs the same opposition between *day* and *night* that Maxi established in his initial questioning of linguistic conventions, but the narrator here, in contrast, appears to have naturalized the accepted relationship between the word and the concept that it signifies: *day* corresponds to *reason* (and, by extension, to *reality*), and *night* to *illusion*. Once again, reason is identified with the acceptance of society's codes, and madness with a deviation from them. The narrator's use of ironic language (circumlocutions and exaggerations such as "la higiene cere-broespinal" and "la espuma que echan de sí las ideas bien batidas"), however, reveals his distance from society's perspective. In reality, he stands apart from Maxi, who now appears to have accepted society's conventions by reestablishing the correspondence between the sign and the referent.[25]

Maxi reasons in the form of deliberate and oftentimes absurd syllogisms, which parody the structure of logical discourse. On one occasion, he overcomes his impulse to search for Fortunata at the Cava de San Miguel by manipulating the language of logic: "Voy a casa, y han dado ya las diez... Luego no debo detenerme" (I'm going home, and it's already ten o'clock... Therefore I shouldn't stop; 2:928). The syllogistic process normally involves the drawing of a conclusion from two premises that have a common middle term. Here, however, any kind of true reasoning becomes lost in the *language* of logical argumentation: the two premises do not have a common middle term, nor does the conclusion logically result from the first two propositions. Ultimately, Maxi's syllogisms become a linguistic game through which he tries to reintegrate himself into society.[26] (The etymology of the word *syllogism* is in itself significant: it combines the Greek *syn* [together] and *logos* [word].) His "reason" is yet another fiction that he invents through his manipulation of language.

During one of his moments of greatest semiotic consciousness, Maxi reflects upon the creative nature of his logic. He explicitly compares

25. Key writings on the ironic use of language in Galdós's works include Engler, *The Structure of Realism*, 56–60; Nimetz, *Humor in Galdós*, 79–106; and Urey, *Galdós and the Irony of Language*.

26. The *Oxford English Dictionary* gives a secondary definition of *syllogism* as "a subtle or tricky speech; a poser; more widely, an artifice, trick" (358–59).

himself to the figure of the poet and attributes the origin of his "reason" to a state of poetic inspiration: "Lo que fulminó en mi cabeza como un resplandor siniestro del delirio, ahora clarea como luz cenital que ilumina todas las cosas. Vaya, hasta poeta me estoy volviendo" (What flashed through my mind like a sinister resplendence in my delirium is now becoming clear, like a light from a high peak that illuminates everything. Well now, I'm even becoming a poet; 2:923). Yet in the same breath, he rejects the idea of poetic inspiration as contrary to logic, as a manifestation of madness: "Pero dejémonos de poesía. La inspiración poética es un estado insano. Lógica, lógica, y nada más que lógica" (But let's forget about poetry; poetic inspiration is an insane state. Logic, logic, and nothing but logic; 2:923). Maxi's thoughts reveal an ambivalence between the autonomous language of poetry, which society associates with madness, and the language of "logic" according to which sanity is defined. He ultimately acknowledges the inseparability of the processes of reasoning and creation:

Es que la inspiración poética precede siempre a la verdad, y antes que la verdad aparezca, traída por la sana lógica, es revelada por la poesía, estado morboso... En fin, que yo lo adiviné, y ahora lo sé. El calor se transforma en fuerza. La poesía se convierte en razón. (2:923)

(Poetic inspiration always precedes truth, and before truth can appear, brought forth by a healthy logic, it's revealed by poetry, a morbid state... In short, I guessed it, and now I know. Heat is transformed into energy. Poetry becomes reason.)

The blurring of the line between sanity and madness, truth and fiction, constitutes the paradox of his "reason of unreason." His syllogisms, which form a part of his fiction, ironically become the means by which he discovers the truth about Fortunata's condition and whereabouts.

The fictionality of Maxi's reason becomes increasingly apparent as he begins to employ "logic" in order to justify his desires. For example, in a symbolic scene, as he contemplates the "mala pájara" (evil bird) that evokes Fortunata's memory, he implicitly justifies the necessity of his wife's death by appealing to the language of "reason." "La lógica exige su muerte," he says to himself, referring at once to the bird and to his wife. "Si siguiera viviendo, no se cumpliría la ley de la razón" (Logic demands her death . . . If she continued to live, the laws of reason would not be obeyed; 2:926).[27] His need to transform the language of reason according to his own desires suggests that he is moving away, once again, from society.

When society's laws fail to defend Maxi's desires, his identification of reason and society collapses. The first major crisis of his "reason" occurs when he discovers Aurora's amorous relationship with Juanito Santa Cruz, violator of his own honor. "Esto lo tolera y aun lo aplaude la sociedad... Luego es una sociedad que no tiene vergüenza," he exclaims to himself, making use of syllogistic language once again. "¿Y qué defensa hay contra esto? En las leyes, ninguna" (Society tolerates and even applauds this... Therefore, society is shameless. And what defense is there against this? In the laws, there's none; 2:929). What Aurora comes to personify, in Maxi's view, is the totality of all feminine disloyalty that he sees society as tolerating. When he recognizes society's "unreason," he decides to act according to a personal sense of justice ("un sentimiento quijotesco de la Justicia" [a quixotic sense of Justice; 2:929]) that is independent of the norms of society. The conflict between society and reason leads Maxi to experience a moment of interpretive crisis. He begins to doubt his own perception, which has led him to question society, as he associates the questioning of society's laws with his former state of "madness":

¿Es verdad que les he visto, al infame y a ella, o lo he soñado? Que yo he tenido un sopor breve y profundo es indudable. Pues ya voy creyendo que ha sido sueño... Sí, sueño ha sido... Aurora es honrada. Vaya con las cosas que sueña uno... Pero no, Dios, si lo vi, si lo vi, si lo estoy viendo todavía, y si tengo estampadas aquí las dos figuras... Esto es para volverse uno loco... , ¡y sería lástima ahora que estoy tan cuerdo! (2:929–30)

(Is it true that I really saw them, the scoundrel and her, or did I dream it? It's beyond doubt that I've dozed off into a brief but profound sleep. Well now I'm beginning to think that it was a dream... Yes, it had to be a dream... Aurora is decent. Look at the things one dreams... But no, by God, I saw it, I saw it, I'm still seeing it, and I have the two figures

27. Several critics have studied the importance of bird symbolism in *Fortunata y Jacinta,* especially in relation to Fortunata (Gilman, "The Birth of Fortunata"; Agnes Gullón, "The Bird Motif and the Introductory Motif: Structure in *Fortunata y Jacinta*"; Utt, " 'El pájaro voló': observaciones sobre un leitmotif en *Fortunata y Jacinta*").

engraved here in my mind... This is enough to drive one crazy... , and it
would be such a pity, now that I'm so sane!)

By considering his perception of reality to be a dream, Maxi attempts to
reconcile the conflict that he sees between reason and society. When
Aurora's *deshonradez* is confirmed and he recognizes the irreconcilability
of this conflict, he has no choice but to abandon society once again.

In his second, more profound rupture with society, Maxi rejects the
"absolute" reason of society and adopts a relative one that serves his
own desires: "Ahora no me basta con la lógica, necesito ver algo más..."
(Logic isn't enough for me any more, I need to see something more... ;
2:930). He gains a greater consciousness of the inseparability of logic
and fiction, a knowledge that is already implicit in his previous reflection upon the creative process. Yet, at the same time, he continues to
manipulate the language of reason. He no longer faces a choice between
madness and society, since his new quixotic logic allows him to stand at
once within and outside the social construct. Those to whom he affirms
his "reason," including the reader, are unable to decide whether he is
mad or sane. Fortunata herself, sharing society's view at this moment,
senses the ambiguity of her husband's logic as she asks herself: "Eso que
dice, ¿es razón, o los mayores disparates que en mi vida le he oído?" (Is
what he's saying reason, or is it the greatest nonsense I've ever heard in
my life?; 2:941). Through his new fiction, Maxi transforms himself into
a saint, superior to society, and a shift in narrative technique helps to
produce the illusion that he has achieved authorial control over his
fiction. Up to this moment, the narrator has frequently offered his
ironic perspective on Maxi's inner thoughts. Now the reader sees him
almost exclusively through the character's external speech without the
explicit intervention of the narrator. Maxi appears to have gained autonomous control over his word.

With quixotic reasoning that allows him to see himself as the de-
fender of justice, Maxi justifies his desire to take revenge on Fortunata:
"Si la mato no hay lección. La enseñanza es más cristiana que la
muerte, quizá más cruel, y de seguro más lógica... Que viva para que
padezca y padeciendo aprenda..." (If I kill her there won't be any
lesson. Teaching is more Christian than death, more cruel, perhaps,
and certainly more logical... Let her live so she'll suffer, and suffering,
let her learn... ; 2:930). His new command of language enables him to
manipulate the object of his desire, setting in motion a chain of events

that eventually leads to his wife's death. As Ricardo Gullón has observed, Maxi ultimately destroys Fortunata with the word.[28] Having become the victim of Maxi's wounding words, Fortunata herself acknowledges the destructive power of his language: "Tú me quieres matar, y en vez de pegarme un tiro, me vienes con esta historia" (You want to kill me, and instead of shooting me you come with this story; 2:943). His ability to wield language as a weapon is significant, given his former incapacity to use words even in self-defense. His power over the word, however, meets its final crisis when Fortunata turns his own language against him. "Has perdido la condición de hombre," she exclaims to her husband, referring at once to his self-transformation into a saint and to the condition of sexual impotence that lies at the root of his fiction, "y no tienes... , vamos al decir, amor propio ni dignidad... Conque ahí tienes tu lección. Aguanta y vuelve por otra. ¿Qué creías? ¿Que yo iba a sufrirte tus lecciones y no te iba a dar las mías?" (You've lost your condition of being a man and you don't have... , well, pride or dignity... So there's a lesson for you. Take it and come back for another one. What did you think, that I was going to put up with your lessons and not give you mine?; 2:958).[29] Fortunata incites the desire that lies hidden beneath her husband's "reason" by promising to love him if he kills Juanito and Aurora for her. Through this act, she causes Maxi's final abandonment of "reason" and his plunge into another form of "madness."

Having been the central presence in these last chapters, Maxi disappears from the pages after his final confrontation with his wife and does not regain his word until Ballester visits him with notice of Fortunata's death. During this time, the narrator refers to him only once, through Doña Lupe's perspective. Maxi's ultimate failure to control his fiction of reason and his sudden absence from the text correspond to his literal loss of the word. After his encounter with Fortunata, he temporarily becomes deprived of his capacity for human speech. He spends the days

28. *Técnicas de Galdós*, 154.

29. If "logocentrism colludes with phallocentrism," as some feminist critics claim (Toril Moi, *Sexual/Textual Politics*, 105), male impotence logically corresponds to the loss of language. The phallus is no longer the privileged signifier. (For Lacan's treatment of "the signification of the phallus," see *Écrits*, 281–91.) From a more traditional angle, Vernon Chamberlin studies two archetypal symbols—water and the windmill—in connection with Maxi's sexual dysfunction ("Poor Maxi's Windmill: Aquatic Symbolism in *Fortunata y Jacinta*").

in solitary confinement, emitting animal-like sounds: his "aullidos" (howls), arbitrary speech acts, have replaced the meaningful word, which has been so potent in his hands before. Segismundo Ballester places his finger on the exact nature of Maxi's new "madness" as he reproachingly exclaims to the fellow pharmacist: "Qué, ¿ha perdido el uso de la palabra?" (What is it? Have you lost the use of words?; 2:978).[30] Maxi, whose "madness" has been based all along on his invention of fictional worlds through linguistic manipulation, now abandons language altogether, thus reaching greater depths of madness in the eyes of society (as is evident from the perspective of Doña Lupe and Ballester).

Maxi is never quite able to free himself from the language of society while he believes Fortunata to be alive. Desire, which originally motivates his semiotic disjunction, paradoxically ties the individual to society and the word to the world, for it can be fulfilled only in the world. When Ballester breaks the news of Fortunata's death to him, Maxi momentarily revives his "reason" in an attempt to prove that his wife is still alive: "¿Apostamos a que con mi lógica vuelvo a descubrir dónde está? ¡Ay Dios mío!, ya siento la lógica invadiendo mi cabeza con fuerza admirable, y el talento vuelve... , sí, me vuelve, aquí está, le siento entrar" (How much do you want to bet that with my logic I'll discover where she is again? Oh, good God! I can already feel logic invading my mind with admirable force, and my talent is returning... , yes, it's returning to me, here it is, I feel it coming; 2:979). His half-hearted return to "reason" represents the final effort to invent a reality that conforms to his desire. Yet he ultimately faces the reality of Fortunata's death when he sees her name on the gravestone. Ironically, it is the written word that brings him back to the real world. For once, he does not question the conventional sign: he reads the inscription on the tombstone as a fixed text that signifies an absolute and final absence, death. The words *de Rubín*, which follow Fortunata's own name, add a further irony, for Maxi, neither as husband nor as author of fictions, has ever "possessed" Fortunata completely: he has never had authority over her. On the other hand, Maxi, through the word, has created a fictional presence, which has had the power to transform his sense of reality.

30. Michel Foucault, who traces the history of madness in Western civilization, characterizes madness by its "fundamental absence of language" (*Madness and Civilization: A History of Insanity in the Age of Reason*, 287). Maxi's silence in *Fortunata y Jacinta* can be seen as a metaphor for the stifled voice of the madman, the language that society tries to deny him.

Maxi gains a new consciousness of his former "madness" after he comes to terms with the death of his desired object. He relinquishes all of his previous fictions as false semiotic systems and acknowledges that he has opposed Nature by creating an arbitrary sign out of Fortunata. According to his new vision, Fortunata, the sign he has fabricated, escapes from his authority because she has been taken out of her "natural" state. With apparent lucidity, he confesses his mistake: "No contamos con la Naturaleza, que es la gran madre y maestra que rectifica los errores de sus hijos extraviados. Nosotros hacemos mil disparates, y la Naturaleza nos los corrige" (We didn't take Nature into account, the great mother and teacher who rectifies the errors of her children who've gone astray. We do countless foolish things, and Nature corrects them; 2:980). In reality, the idea of the natural sign, exemplified in the identification between Fortunata and Nature, is a myth that Maxi invents in order to explain what he perceives to be his failure as a creator of signs. If one were to posit an authentic language of Nature, both Maxi and society would be placed on an equal plane in their creation of arbitrary systems of signs.

For Maxi, a true reconciliation between language and Nature, fiction and reality, is impossible. Instead of reconstructing Fortunata in her "natural" state, he once again transforms her into a pure ideal:

> declaro que quiero a mi mujer lo mismo que el día en que la conocí; adoro en ella lo ideal, lo eterno, y la veo, no como era, sino tal y como yo la soñaba y la veía en mi alma . . . Ahora que no vive, la contemplo libre de las transformaciones que el mundo y el contacto del mal le imprimían . . . desaparecieron las asquerosidades de la realidad, y vivo con mi ídolo en mi idea, y nos adoramos con pureza y santidad sublimes en el tálamo incorruptible de mi pensamiento. (2:980)

> (I declare that I love my wife as much as the day I met her; I adore what is ideal and eternal in her, and I see her not as she was, but rather as I dreamed and envisioned her in my soul . . . Now that she's no longer alive, I contemplate her, freed from the transformations that the world and contact with evil impressed upon her . . . the disgusting side of reality has disappeared, and I live with my idol in my idea, and we adore each other with sublime purity and saintliness in the incorruptible nuptial chamber of my thought.)

Maxi's coming to terms with Fortunata's death and with the impossibility of ever fulfilling his desire in the world enables him to free his fiction completely. He has achieved the true state of *Pensamiento puro*, which is only possible when the referent of his desire no longer binds him to the world. He renounces society and chooses his own "madness," recognizing it as such. This time he no longer feels the need to free the entire society from its false system of signs: he aspires only to his own liberation.

At this point, Maxi expresses his wish to enter a monastery, knowing that he will be taken to the insane asylum. The euphemism of the "monastery" is significant as the mystical experience becomes a metaphor for the freeing of language from the world. His final words upon entering Leganés reveal that he is withdrawing from society voluntarily with a full consciousness of his own transcendence. He no longer addresses society as he did before in the café but pronounces these words as if he were speaking to an invisible being:

> —¡Si creerán estos tontos que me engañan! Esto es Leganés. Lo acepto, lo acepto y me callo, en prueba de la sumisión absoluta de mi voluntad a lo que el mundo quiera hacer de mi persona. No encerrarán entre murallas mi pensamiento. Resido en las estrellas. Pongan al llamado Maximiliano Rubín en un palacio o en un muladar..., lo mismo da. (2:981)

> (Why, these fools think they're deceiving me! This is Leganés. I accept it, I accept it in silence, to prove the absolute submission of my will to whatever the world wishes to do with my person. They won't confine my thought within these walls. I reside in the stars. Let them put the so-called Maximiliano Rubín in a palace or a dung heap... it's all the same.)

Maxi asserts his superiority over the others ("estos tontos"), who are still tied to society's codes. He, for his part, lives in the ethereal realm of the stars, freed from the world. He refers to himself alternately in first-person and third-person form, as if he were two separate beings. The "yo" is the true self, represented by his "pensamiento"; "mi persona" and "el llamado Maximiliano Rubín" refer to the other "false" self that exists only for the world. The use of the adjective *llamado* in this context suggests the character's rejection of the name and identity that society has given him. (The sign *Maximiliano*, etymologically related to the word *máximo*, is ironic while the reader shares society's viewpoint, but it loses this irony in the context of Maxi's ultimate transcendence.) Maxi's final assertion ("Pongan al llamado Maximiliano Rubín en un palacio o en un muladar... lo mismo da"), also the concluding words of the novel, represents the ultimate affirmation of the state of *Pensamiento puro* that he has achieved. The words *palacio* and *muladar*, which signify opposite realities for society, are the same for Maxi, who sees them as autonomous signifiers. By freeing himself from society, he has, in his mind, freed language from the world.

From the moment of his initial appearance to his final exit from the novel, Maxi is engaged in a struggle with the problems of language. His recognition of the arbitrariness of the sign, which comes as a result of his disjunction from society's codes, allows him to manipulate language in order to create fictional worlds. As interpreter and creator of signs, he constantly oscillates between his own fictions and those of society. First, he manipulates the sign from within the conventions of society in order to produce a desired referent; he then seeks to free the sign from the referent through his mystical philosophy. The failure of his fictional theology forces him to return to society with his "reason," which represents yet another construct of language. Finally, Fortunata's death—the death of the referent—allows him to withdraw from society altogether and to escape into pure fiction. His creative activity comes to a standstill as soon as he detaches his fiction completely from a referent in the real world. Galdós's novel and Maxi's fiction come together at their conclusion. Once the "madman" liberates the sign and fiction becomes nothing but fiction, it loses its reason for being: the novel must end at this moment. The disappearance of the narrator, who yields the final word to Maxi, confirms the character's privileged place in the work as a whole.

Maximiliano Rubín's role in the text as a reader and creator of signs calls attention to his own identity as a sign: he is, to borrow Felman's words, "a sign that generates other signs."[31] At the same time, the conventions of realist fiction allow these signs to take on the quality of "the real," "the having-been-there of things," as Barthes would say.[32] Ultimately, Maxi's struggle with the sign dramatizes the confrontation between two opposing tendencies of the novel: the impulse toward rep-

---

31. In her analysis of "The Illustrious Gaudissart," Felman thus characterizes the madman. According to her, the madman's discourse points self-reflexively to "the dynamics of a language game," rather than to a referent in the real world (*Writing and Madness*, 110).

32. "The Reality Effect," in *The Rustle of Language*, 141–48.

resentation and the opposing tendency to assert its autonomy as language. For Felman, the madness of literature lies precisely in its resistance to meaning: "[it] consists neither in *sense* nor in *non-sense*: it is not a final *signified* . . . it is rather a kind of *rhythm*; a rhythm that is unpredictable, incalculable, unsayable, but that is nonetheless fundamentally narratable as the story of the slippage of a reading between the excessive fullness and the excessive emptiness of meaning."[33] *Fortunata y Jacinta*, by dramatizing this textual madness through Maxi's semiotic struggle, engages itself in a constant process of self-reflection.

33. *Writing and Madness*, 254.

2

The Myth of the Natural Sign
in *El doctor Centeno*

Felipe's Faith in Language

Semiotic preoccupations are central in *Fortunata y Jacinta*, as the linguistic nature of Maximiliano Rubín's "madness" demonstrates. The contradictory impulses that guide Maxi's struggle with language reveal the basic linguistic paradigm behind Galdós's discourse. Although the tension between two different theories of language characterizes the discourse of the implied author (or sometimes, of the narrator), individual characters within Galdós's works often engage in the act of interpretation with a belief in a particular vision of the sign. Such is the case in *El doctor Centeno*, one of the earlier and less studied of the *Novelas españolas contemporáneas*.

The protagonist of the novel, Felipe Centeno, attempts to come to terms with the problems of language as he searches for knowledge. In contrast to Maxi, who strives to free language from the world through an awareness of the arbitrariness of the sign, Felipe seeks to discover a referent behind the signs of the world. The implicit notion of language that underlies his search for knowledge is the belief in the capacity of the sign to represent reality and, consequently, to lead him to the truth. Felipe's belief in "natural language" is continually challenged by society's deceptive signs and especially by his contact with his two masters, Pedro Polo and Alejandro Miquis, each of whom represents a more complex vision of the sign.[1] Although Felipe, through his apprenticeship with Polo and Miquis, learns to manipulate the sign to a certain extent, his initiation into the worlds of his masters remains incomplete. In the end, having failed to join society by mastering its semiotic con-

---

1. Roland Barthes defines "natural" language as a "language which feigns ignorance of the fact of its nature as language," that is, of the fact that it is a function of a particular semiological system (*Image-Music-Text*, 199). "Natural" language, which, according to Barthes, forms the basis of myth, posits a motivated link between the signifier and the signified, the form and the meaning, when in reality this relation is arbitrary (*Mythologies*, 109–31).

ventions, like Polo, or to escape into the realm of autonomous poetic
language, like Miquis, Felipe emerges with a reaffirmation of his original faith in language. His struggle to overcome the arbitrariness of the
sign therefore provides the novel as a whole with a coherent trajectory.[2]

Felipe's vision of the sign, which represents a naive "realism," presumes that language corresponds naturally to a referent behind it. The
implied author, however, exposes the conventionality of such a notion of
"realism" (or of the "real") by setting the protagonist in conflict with
other voices in the text, whether these voices belong to other characters
or to the narrator himself.[3] The opposing theory, which challenges
Felipe's "realist" vision, considers the sign to be arbitrary and therefore
independent from a fixed referent. *El doctor Centeno* dramatizes the
confrontation between these two conceptions of the sign through Felipe's
struggle with the signs of the world around him and through the narrator's ironic attitude toward this struggle.

The novel begins as a parody of an epic convention, as the narrator
introduces the yet-unnamed protagonist in a mock-heroic tone:

2. The question of the novel's "unity" has engaged the attention of critics since
José F. Montesinos. As the first of several *galdosistas* to address this problem, Montesinos launches a critical debate by suggesting the work's apparent lack of unity: "*El
doctor Centeno* es una novela extraordinariamente fluida, rebelde a fraguar en un
molde único. Es parte de un ciclo novelesco, aunque el autor parece por momentos
no darse cuenta de ello. O más bien diríamos: es 'partes', no 'parte', de un ciclo,
pues se nos antoja fusión de dos novelas" (*El doctor Centeno* is an extraordinarily fluid
novel, resistant to setting in a single mold. It forms a part of a novelistic cycle,
although the author, at times, doesn't seem to realize it. Or rather, we should say: it
forms "parts," not "a part" of a cycle since we have the notion that it is a fusion of two
novels; *Galdós*, 62). Germán Gullón responds to Montesinos's statement by demon-
strating that the novel does indeed have unity: he stresses the unifying function of
Felipe Centeno's development ("el hacerse del protagonista" [the self-formation of
the protagonist]) and of the protagonist's consciousness, through which the events
are filtered ("Unidad de *El doctor Centeno*," 548). Other critics have reacted to Montesinos's declaration from a primarily sociological perspective. Gloria Moreno Castillo considers the themes of education and culture as providing unity to the novel
("La unidad de tema en *El doctor Centeno*"). Geraldine Scanlon, for her part, asserts
that all of the work's major themes are related to "the crisis of values in a society
which was undergoing significant economic and political change" ("*El doctor Centeno*: A Study in Obsolescent Values," 245).

3. Roland Barthes explores the convention that produces the "reality effect"
("the *having-been-there* of things"), which he defines in semiotic terms as "the *direct*
collusion of a referent and a signifier," whereby the signified, or the narrative structure itself, is expelled from the sign (*The Rustle of Language*, 147).

Con paso decidido acomete el héroe la empinada Cuesta del Obser-
vatorio. Es, para decirlo pronto, un héroe chiquito, paliducho, mal dota-
do de carnes y peor de vestido con que cubrirlas; tan insignificante, que
ningún transeúnte, de éstos que llaman personas, puede creer, al verle,
que es de heroico linaje y de casta de inmortales, aunque no esté destinado a arrojar un nombre más en el enorme y ya sofocante inventario
de las celebridades humanas. (1:1312)

(With a determined stride, the hero rushes upon the steep slope of the
Observatory. He is, to be brief, a tiny and palish hero, ill-equipped with
flesh, and, even worse, with dress to cover it; he's so insignificant that no
passer-by, of those called personages, would believe, upon seeing him,
that he is of heroic lineage and of a caste of immortals, although he might
not be destined to hurl yet another name upon the already enormous and
stifling inventory of human feats.)

The character appears here as an insignificant "antihero," set in direct
contrast to the image of the traditional epic hero. Later in the same
chapter, the narrator persists in his travesty of the heroic quest as he
compares Felipe's struggle with his first cigar, the most mundane of
experiences, to the epic hero's combat with a titanic monster:

Un papelillo entero de mixto se consume en la empresa incendiaria;
pero al fin el héroe tiene el gusto de ver quemada y humeante la cola del
monstruo. Este se defiende con ferocidad de las quijadas, que remedan
los fuelles de Vulcano. Lucha desesperada, horrible, titánica. (1:1314)

(An entire paper-roll of matches is consumed in the incendiary under-
taking; but at last the hero has the pleasure of seeing the monster's tail
burnt and smoldering. He defends himself with the ferocity of his jaws,
which mimic Vulcan's bellows. Desperate struggle, horrible and titanic.)

The use of parody, as Hutcheon has observed, is closely linked to the
self-reflexive role of the literary text.[4] Parodic devices unmask and
critique the inadequacies of a certain literary convention at the same
time as they rework and reinterpret these conventions in a self-conscious

---

4. *Narcissistic Narrative*, 49–53. For a more extensive discussion of parody and its
function in self-conscious art, see Hutcheon's *A Theory of Parody*.

way. Galdós's novel, by parodying a high literary style, may at first seem to defend a "realist" style and conception of literature in which the supposed imitation of everyday, even mundane reality, rather than the invention of singular deeds, forms the basis of literary narration. This apparent movement toward a "realist" credo that posits a mimetic relationship between the linguistic sign and its referent is, however, made ambiguous by the use of parodic language, which lays bare the disjunction between words and the reality behind them. Galdós's text paradoxically makes use of the very elements that it purportedly parodies. Parody, rather than replacing one convention with another in a hierarchical manner, calls attention to the conventionality of all forms of discourse. The naive ideal of "realist" discourse, represented by Felipe Centeno's vision of the sign, is no exception.

Similarly, in the second paragraph, the narrator employs a deliberately ironic language that undermines his own declaration:

> Esto no impide que [Felipe] ocupe ya sobre el regazo de la madre Naturaleza el lugar que le corresponde, y que respire, ande y desempeñe una y otra función vital con el alborozo y brío de todo ser que estrena sus órganos. (1:1313)

> (This doesn't prevent him [Felipe] from occupying the place that belongs to him on mother Nature's lap, and from breathing, walking, and carrying out one or other of his vital functions with the joy and spirit of all those who use their organs for the first time.)

On the one hand, the narrator appears to establish an identification between Felipe and nature. Nevertheless, his continued use of the mock heroic tone and of circumlocutory language (especially the indirect, double-negative "no impide" at the beginning of the sentence) calls into question the reliability of his discourse. By ironically associating Felipe with nature, the narrator simultaneously anticipates the protagonist's belief in the natural sign and exposes this vision of the sign to be a myth.

Felipe's conception of the sign inevitably conflicts with the codes of society, which are always deceptive: the social sign asserts a natural link to a referent when, in reality, this connection is arbitrary. In *El doctor Centeno*, as in a number of other novels by Galdós, the city, which stands opposed to nature and thus represents a more complex vision of the sign, becomes associated with a proliferation of semiotic activity.[5] Felipe's disjunction from the social codes of the city both stimulates and frustrates his quest for truth. His repeated attempts to decipher the signs of the world around him are reminiscent of Manolo Infante's interpretive frenzy in *La incógnita* (Chapter 4). The city is linked to hypocrisy and the cult of appearances, themes which recur in Galdós's works. In *La de Bringas*, Rosalía de Bringas pawns her possessions and ultimately prostitutes herself in order to maintain the external appearance of economic well-being. The three "Miaus" in *Miau* and Doña Paca in *Misericordia* likewise squander what little money they have in order to project the appearance of material comfort to the rest of society.

In contrast to these characters, who live within the conventions of society, Felipe's position as an outsider allows him to sense the gap between his innocence and the complexity of social codes. Believing that an initiation into middle-class society will lead him to the truth, he begins his own "education" by manipulating the sign from within the social construct. At the beginning of the novel, Felipe deliberately engages in a social act, the smoking of a cigar. The narrator mocks the character's naive vision of the social sign: "piensa mi hombre que fumarse ricamente un puro es cosa también muy conforme con el señorío" (my man thinks that smoking a cigar opulently is also a thing that goes with being an important man; 1:1314). Felipe's semiotic activity is reminiscent of Maximiliano Rubín's effort to produce a true "honradez del alma" in *Fortunata* by creating the social appearance of *honradez* (Chapter 1).

Felipe Centeno's initiation into society takes a specifically linguistic form. In his first verbal exchange upon entering the city, he literally deconstructs language by adding the prefix *des-* to certain words. The distortion of language symbolically marks his introduction into a deceptive world where signs never mean what they seem to say. Through his manipulation of language, the protagonist seeks to become a part of the

---

5. Alter examines the centrality of the city topos in the nineteenth-century realist novel in connection with what he considers to be the eclipse of the self-conscious novel during this period. According to Alter, novel writing in the nineteenth century primarily represents "a means of containing the mounting chaos of the contemporary world," especially the chaos of the emergent metropolis. An awareness of the novel's artificiality, he believes, would undermine its project of outdoing "a threatening or at least bewildering historical reality by remaking it" (*Partial Magic*, 93, 97). Galdós's novels, however, implicitly call attention to the linguistic nature of realist discourse by presenting the chaos of the Spanish metropolis as a semiotic phenomenon.

bourgeois society of the metropolis. Yet by adding *des-* to these words, he affirms the exact contrary of what he means to say and further marginalizes himself from society. It is, then, doubly ironical that the innocent Felipe unintentionally lays bare the duplicity of the social sign. In his first dialogue with Alejandro Miquis, Felipe declares that he has come to the city in order to *desaprender* (unlearn) and later confuses the words *destruir* (destroy) and *instruir* (instruct; 1:1317). His linguistic blunders are absurd from society's perspective, but within the larger context of the novel, they expose the destructive nature of the established educational system. The individual who seeks true knowledge can attain it only through the complete *unlearning* of social language (that is, through a *des-educación*). Yet the very notion of a truth behind the social construct is and will always be a myth: Felipe Centeno's quest is therefore destined to fail.

A number of critics have noted the centrality of the theme of education in *El doctor Centeno*.[6] The first two sections are entitled, respectively, "Introducción a la pedagogía" (Introduction to pedagogy) and "Pedagogía" (Pedagogy). On one level, the novel contains a critique of an educational system that serves to initiate the individual into the false semiotic system of society. As Jesús Delgado (one of the boarders of Doña Virginia's *pensión*) affirms, education fails in this society because it fails to develop authentic signification, that is, a true correspondence between knowledge and truth. In one of his letters to himself, he declares that the educational institution, which privileges the *parecer* over the *ser*, reflects the values of society itself.[7] Delgado, who advocates a pedagogy that has direct relevance to the individual's experience, remains trapped within a solipsistic world because his ideal can never be reconciled with social reality: he has no choice but to withdraw into his *eautepistolografía* (auto-epistolography).[8]

6. See Peter Bly, *Galdós's Novel of the Historical Imagination*; Denah Lida, "Sobre el 'krausismo' de Galdós"; Moreno Castillo, "La unidad de tema."

7. Denah Lida stresses the importance of Jesús Delgado's function in the novel as a spokesperson for the educational philosophy of two influential Krausist thinkers of the time: Sanz del Río and his disciple, Francisco Giner de los Ríos ("Sobre el 'krausismo' "). Geraldine Scanlon, along the same line, considers the positivist philosopher Herbert Spencer to be a greater influence on Delgado. Spencer's attitude toward educational progress, according to Scanlon, is closely allied to Galdós's own ideas (*"El doctor Centeno"*).

8. The failure of pedagogical theory is also one theme of *El amigo Manso*, another work that concerns itself simultaneously with education and fictional creation (see Kronik's *"El amigo Manso* and the Game of Fictive Autonomy"). Máximo Manso,

Pedro Polo's pedagogical method, characterized by the narrator as "una operación *inyecto-cerebral*" (an operation of cerebral injection; 1:1331), epitomizes this false education in which "knowledge" has no bearing on the truth: it is a symptom of society itself, which, by definition, is a construct of language behind which there is no truth. Polo's upward mobility and apparent success in such a society are due precisely to his ability to manipulate its deceptive signs. Teacher and preacher by profession, Polo is endowed with the gift of the word. His sermons, a pastiche of various texts, are entirely vacuous in content, yet through his "pico de oro" (golden tongue; 1:1333, 1341) he is able to create the illusion of a link between his signifiers and a corresponding meaning that does not really exist. His ability to deceive through his linguistic talent is inseparable from his pedagogical role within society.[9]

As Felipe Centeno enters Polo's service, the latter's mastery of the sign is contrasted with his servant's semiotic innocence. Felipe fails as a student in Polo's institution because he cannot learn to understand and to manipulate the duplicitous signs of society. Significantly, one of the few subjects that attracts him is geography, which communicates knowledge through the map, a special form of the motivated sign. To borrow a term originally employed by Charles Peirce, the map is an icon, a sign that represents its object through an actual resemblance.[10] The map is comprehensible to Felipe only because it is analogous to the reality that

---

like Jesús Delgado, is unable to reconcile the language of society with that of his own fictions.

9. Polo's free-floating signifiers are reminiscent of Torquemada's equally vacuous oration, which represents the culmination of his linguistic transformation in *Torquemada en el purgatorio*. As Torquemada gloats over the seductive power of his language, he declares: "Mi discurso no fue más que una *serie no interrumpida* de vaciedades, cuatro frases que recogí de los periódicos, alguna que otra expresioncilla que se me pegó en el Senado y otras tantas migajas del buen decir de nuestro amigo Donoso. Con todo ello hice una ensalada… Vamos, si aquello no tenía pies ni cabeza… , y lo fui soltando conforme se me iba ocurriendo. ¡Vaya con el efecto que causaba!" ("My speech was nothing but an *uninterrupted series* of empty phrases, a few sentences I picked up from the newspapers, one or another little expression that stuck to me in the Senate, and a few other bits of good sayings from our friend Donoso. I made a salad out of all that… Heavens, it made no sense at all… , and I let it out as it occurred to me. What an effect it caused!"; 2:1540). Yet another Galdosian character gifted with "el extraordinario hechizo de la palabra" (an extraordinary charm with words) is Manolo Peña (*El amigo Manso*), who, as he gives a speech on charity, is able to captivate his audience with empty words (1:1253).

10. "Logic as Semiotic: The Theory of Signs," 10. I am making isolated use of Peirce's term for convenience. I do not propose to adopt his entire semiotic system.

it represents. Conversely, he is unable to comprehend any kind of symbolic language in which the connection between the sign and the referent is not self-evident. Thus, it is not surprising that grammar is among his weakest subjects:

> No son para contados los testimonios que levantaba y los trastrueques que hacía al intentar decir que "el participio es una parte de la oración que participa en la índole del verbo y del adjetivo." En otras definiciones se trabucaba más por no conocer el valor y significado de las palabras. (1:1336)

> (It's impossible to count how many testimonies he brought to bear and how many mistakes he made in trying to say: "the participle is a part of a sentence that forms a part of the class of both the verb and the adjective." He jumbled other definitions even more by not knowing the value and meaning of words.)

Felipe Centeno is incapable of manipulating metalanguage, which serves not to imitate "nature" but to interpret language itself.[11]

Outside of Pedro Polo's institution, Felipe Centeno comes into contact with another character, Juanito del Socorro, who unsuccessfully tries to initiate him into society. Characterized by the narrator as "más embustero que el inventor de las mentiras" (a greater liar than the inventor of lies), he becomes a symbolic father figure for Felipe, who is unwise to the ways of the world ("dándose aires de protector, [Juanito] llamaba a su amigo *hijito*" [putting on airs as a protector, Juanito called his friend *my son*; 1:1340]). It is appropriate that Juanito works as a messenger boy for a printing office, where the word reigns supreme. Like Pedro Polo, the corrupt Juanito has mastered the art of linguistic deception: he constructs elaborate narratives ("maravillosas historias" [wondrous stories]), blatant lies, in order to win his companion's admiration (1:1353). Juanito, who recognizes the duplicitous nature of language, uses this knowledge for his own ends. The name "Juanito del Socorro" is itself a deceptive sign: later in the novel, the messenger boy,

11. See Roland Barthes's "Literature and Metalanguage," where *metalanguage* is defined as a symbolic language used to interpret the structure of a real language, or a "language object" (*Critical Essays*, 98).

instead of aiding the destitute Felipe, reduces his friend to a state of drunkenness.

Juanito del Socorro and Pedro Polo are not unique among Galdosian characters in their constant use of language to deceive others. In *Fortunata y Jacinta*, Juanito Santa Cruz, with his linguistic talent, "rewrites" the shameful story that he has inadvertently confessed to Jacinta in a moment of drunkenness.[12] The narrator compares Juanito Santa Cruz's craft with that of a tailor who prepares a garment: "Todo era convencionalismo y frase ingeniosa en aquel hombre que se había emperejilado intelectualmente, cortádose una levita para las ideas y planchándole los cuellos al lenguaje" (Everything was conventional sayings and ingenious phrases about that man, who had dressed himself up in intellectual airs, cutting himself a frock coat from ready-made ideas and ironing the collars of language; 2:498). Implicit in Santa Cruz's deceptive art is the idea that language can replace the "truth" in the same way that clothes make the man. During a confrontation with his wife later in the novel, Juanito Santa Cruz uses his skill as storyteller again ("con aquella presteza de juicio del artista improvisador, hizo su composición" [with the quick judgment of an improvising artist, he laid out his composition]; 2:747), this time in order to justify his second liaison with Fortunata. He inspires Jacinta's pity by recreating the story of Fortunata's life into "una historia de intrigas, violencias y atrocidades" (a story of intrigues, violence and atrocities; 2:747) that conforms to the conventions of the *folletín*. Víctor Cadalso of *Miau* is yet another master of deceptive language: "Aquel hombre, que sabía desplegar tan variados recursos de palabra y de ingenio cuando se proponía mortificar a alguien, . . . entendía maravillosamente el arte de agradar cuando entraba en sus miras" (That man, who knew how to deploy such varied resources of the word and of his ingenuity when he had the intention of mortifying someone, . . . understood wondrously the art of gratifying when it entered into his mind; 2:1020). His knowledge of literary conventions allows him to imitate the language of romantic fiction in an attempt to seduce the unwary Abelarda.

Felipe continues his search for truth behind the signs of society rather than learning to manipulate these signs like many of the other characters. According to their opposing semiotic visions, Felipe and Juanito interpret the social sign in contrary ways: Felipe, in his basic innocence,

12. See John W. Kronik's discussion of Juanito Santa Cruz's key function as storyteller in *Fortunata y Jacinta* ("Narraciones interiores").

sees it as an authentic sign; his worldly-wise companion, in contrast, perceives it as a deceptive one. As the two observe the display window of a jewelry store in the Calle de la Montera, the narrator notes this difference:

> Mirando las joyerías, Felipe, cuyo espíritu generoso se inclinaba siempre al optimismo, sostenía que todo era de ley. Mas para Juanito—alias *Redator*—, que, cual hombre de mundo, se había contaminado del moderno pesimismo, todo era falso. (1:1353)

> (Looking at the jewelry shops, Felipe, whose generous spirit always inclined toward optimism, maintained that everything was genuine. But for Juanito—alias *Redator*—who, as a man of the world, had been contaminated by modern pessimism, everything was fake.)

At one point, Juanito el Socorro exclaims to Felipe, "Tú no tienes mundo" (You're not worldly-wise), upon perceiving his friend's readiness to assume a natural correspondence between a person's external dress and his or her condition of worth (1:1353). The use of the word *mundo* (world) in this context calls attention to the world as a construct, as a product of a convention common to a group of individuals.[13] Felipe's belief in a natural, rather than a conventional, connection between the sign and the referent constitutes his lack of "mundo" or of worldly sophistication.

Felipe's incapacity to recognize the gap between appearance and reality, between signs and their referents, ultimately leads to his dismissal from Pedro Polo's service. After he sees Polo courting Amparo Sánchez y Emperador one evening, he misinterprets his master's subsequent indulgence as a sign of friendship. Juanito del Socorro, who, for his part, is able to discern the reality behind the false appearances of the world, correctly interprets Polo's actions for Felipe: "Que tu amo es un buen peje, y las chicas esas, unas *cursis*" (Your master is a crafty fellow, and those girls are vulgar; 1:1355). Polo's hypocrisy is transparent to Juanito, who also exploits the duplicity of the sign.

13. The dictionary of the Real Academia defines *mundo* as "parte de la sociedad humana, caracterizada por alguna cualidad o circunstancia común a todos sus individuos" (part of human society, characterized by some quality or circumstance that is common to all of its individuals; 1039).

More directly, Felipe's fascination with a sculpted bull's head leads to the loss of his position as Pedro Polo's servant. His childish mischief with this sculpture, which he has found in the convent, provides Polo with a pretext for discharging his servant, who has unknowingly witnessed his rendezvous with "la Emperadora." Ironically, Polo dismisses Felipe because he is unable to conceive of his servant's innocence, when in reality Felipe completely fails to interpret the signs of his master's corruption. The protagonist's innocence is revealed in his inability to distinguish between artifice and "nature." The sculpture, a work of art, allures him with its seemingly perfect reproduction of nature. The narrator, adopting Felipe's viewpoint, declares: "El escultor que lo hizo había sabido imitar a la Naturaleza con tan exquisito arte, que al animal no le faltaba más que mugir" (The sculptor who created it knew how to imitate Nature with such exquisite artistry that the only thing missing from the animal was that it didn't roar; 1:1346). The bull's head, furthermore, is used in a children's game. Felipe's companions simulate a bullfight by staging an intricate representation in which they assume various roles, "picador, caballo, banderillero, mula, toro y diestro" (picador, horse, banderillero, mule, bull, and bullfighter; 1:1344). They rename themselves with aliases in order to assert authority over their fictional world. The children's fiction begins to take on the quality of real life for Felipe, who is later admitted into their game. The narrator himself declares that the children imitate the bull's disembowelment of the horse "con tal arte que parecía que se le salían las tripas y que se las pisaba, como suele suceder a los caballos de verdad en la sangrienta arena de la Plaza" (with such art that it seemed that the entrails were coming out of it and that they were being stepped on, like it often happens to real horses in the bloody arena of the Plaza; 1:1344). Felipe's loss of distance from the world of artifice is reminiscent of the figure of Don Quixote in the Maese Pedro scene. For Felipe, the bull's mask represents a way to further validate the children's fiction. The final destruction of the mask by the policemen and the harsh punishment that Felipe receives from Polo are symbolic of the threat that society poses to the protagonist's innocent vision of the sign.

The third section of the novel, "Quiromancia" (Chiromancy), provides a transition between two stages of Felipe's apprenticeship in society. This apprenticeship occurs under two different masters, Pedro Polo and Alejandro Miquis. After Polo discharges him, the protagonist fortuitously encounters Miquis once again, and this second meeting, which the narrator describes as "prólogo de los importantes acontecimientos que vienen ahora" (prologue to the important events that are now coming; 1:1364), is directly followed by Felipe's errand to the home of Miquis's eccentric aunt, Doña Isabel. Centeno's trip through the labyrinthine streets of Madrid becomes a metaphor for the character's continual search for meaning in a society of duplicitous signs. At the end of the character's journey, as he faces Doña Isabel's house, the narrator declares:

> [La casa] era para él tan misteriosa, emblemática e incomprensible como una de aquellas páginas de la Gramática o de la Aritmética, llenas de definiciones y guarismos que no había entendido nunca. Miraba y miraba, descifrando con el incipiente prurito de su mente investigadora... (1:1366)

> (The house was, for him, as mysterious, emblematic, and incomprehensible as one of those pages of Grammar or Arithmetic, full of definitions and ciphers that he had never understood. He looked and looked, deciphering with the incipient urge of his investigating mind...)

For Felipe, Isabel's house represents a microcosm of the enigmatic world outside. The comparison between the inscrutability of the schoolbooks and that of Isabel's house provides a link between Felipe's formal education in Polo's school and his broader education in society, neither of which is sufficient to change his belief in the possibility of true knowledge.

After he successfully completes his errand to Isabel's house and officially becomes Miquis's servant, Felipe Centeno enters a new stage of his "education" in society. The idealist Manchegan, whom the narrator repeatedly characterizes as a dreamer, evokes the archetypal figure of Don Quixote.[14] At the end of the third section of the novel, the narrator implicitly compares the pair to Don Quixote and Sancho Panza:

> Interesante grupo formaban los dos, el uno come que come y el otro piensa que piensa, soñando de otra manera que Felipe y gastando anticipadamente la vida de los días sucesivos; lanzando su espíritu al por-

---

14. José Luis López Muñoz examines Alejandro Miquis's quixotism and its influence over the basically "realist" Felipe Centeno ("Felipe Centeno, un héroe oscuro e inédito," 254–55).

venir, sus sentidos, a las emociones esperadas, empeñando su voluntad en grandes lides y altísimos propósitos. (1:1383)

(The two formed an interesting group, the one eats and eats, and the other thinks and thinks, dreaming in a different way from Felipe and spending the life of succeeding days in advance; launching his spirit toward the future, his senses toward hoped-for emotions, engaging his will in great combats and lofty aims.)

Despite their apparent difference, however, Miquis and Centeno are alike in their condition of alienation from society. As the narrator declares: "Siendo tan diferentes, algo les era común: el entusiasmo, quizás la inocencia" (Being so different, they had something in common: their enthusiasm, perhaps their innocence; 1:1396). Both characters, at odds with the world, attempt to close the distance between the self and the world in their opposing ways: while Felipe searches for a truth behind the social construct, his master seeks to escape from society altogether by inventing his own fiction. In semiotic terms, Felipe endeavors to overcome the arbitrariness of the sign by naturalizing it, in contrast to Alejandro, who struggles to free the sign from its referent.

After Felipe moves into Doña Virginia's boardinghouse with his master, he continues to encounter signs that he is unable to decipher. As he examines the notes of one of the boarders, he discovers a series of mathematical symbols that completely baffle him because of their apparent lack of resemblance to his knowledge of the real world:

El miraba, miraba, volvía páginas, y luego observaba los apuntes que el cadete hacía con lápiz, en los cuales había los mismos signos, la propia mezcolanza de guarismos y letras. A, palito, B; y todo por el estilo. ¿Y aquello era la Matemática? ¿Y para qué servía la Matemática? (1:1391)

(He looked and looked, turned pages, and then observed the notes that the cadet had made in pencil, in which there were the same signs, the same jumble of numbers and letters. A, dash, B; and things like that. And this was Mathematics? And of what use was Mathematics?)

Cienfuegos's anatomy book, on the other hand, inspires a strong curiosity in Felipe, who is fascinated by the direct correspondence between the diagram in the text and the actual parts of his own body. Like the map, the diagram is a sign that is comprehensible to Felipe because of its seemingly direct representation of Nature. His attempt to perform an autopsy on Rosa Ido del Sagrario's cat later in the novel illustrates his desire to verify scientifically the correspondence between the sign (the diagram of anatomical parts) and the referent (the actual anatomical parts in the cat).

Felipe's search for a true referent behind the sign is emblematic of his desire for a knowledge that pertains directly to the experience of everyday reality. This is precisely the ideal of education that Jesús Delgado advocates. For Felipe, science becomes synonymous with nature, scientific knowledge with truth. As he dissects Rosa Ido's cat, he adopts the role of a doctor, a "sabio" (scientist) who searches for the cause of a medical ailment through scientific observation. The title "doctor," originally given to him by the sarcastic Pedro Polo in order to humiliate him, becomes less ironic in the larger context of the novel. The apparent irony of the novel's title is, therefore, double-edged. Other characters truly consider Felipe to be a doctor: Rosa Ido, for example, shows faith in his medical skills by begging him to cure her moribund cat. It is appropriate that the "doctor" comes from the town of Socartes, an anagram for "Sócrates," a name which in turn connotes wisdom and knowledge. Following Felipe's dissection of the cat, Miquis renames his servant "Aristóteles," after the Greek philosopher, as he exclaims: "Eres un sabio y debías llamarte Aristóteles" (You are a wise man and you should be called Aristotle; 1:1440). Finally, even the narrator of the novel begins to refer to the character by this name.

Germán Gullón considers the renaming of Celipín Centeno to be a reflection of the protagonist's development—of his "iluminación progresiva" (progressive enlightenment).[15] In reality, these names ("El doctor Centeno" and "Aristóteles") represent a basically consistent attitude in Felipe throughout his trajectory: his determination to attain true knowledge in a society where the objective of education is *parecer* rather than *ser*. As Barthes asserts in his "Proust and Names," the importance of names lies precisely in this ability to create "a kind of natural affinity between the signifier and signified." What he calls the "hypersemanticity" of names is a manifestation of the writer's ability to invent a completely new reality through language as well as an assertion of his or her authority over this reality.[16] Not only names themselves but

15. "Unidad de *El doctor Centeno*," 584.
16. *New Critical Essays*, 62, 60. Paradoxically, a completely antithetical relation-

also the act of naming assume a central importance in *El doctor Centeno*. For example, Federico Ruiz, an astronomer, poet, and fervent Catholic, questions the mythological names of the celestial bodies and renames them after the patriarchs and saints of the Christian religion. Through this linguistic act, he seeks to reconcile the systems of science and Christianity. Arias Ortiz, another of Doña Virginia's boarders, dubs Jesús Delgado with the Greek name *eautepistológrafos* (auto-epistolographer) in order to capture the enigmatic nature of the latter's epistolary mania (1:1403). As we have already seen, many others, from Felipe's bullfighting companions to Pedro Polo, also engage in the act of naming.

Not surprisingly, Felipe Centeno's belief in natural language corresponds to his naive conception of literature as the direct representation of truth. He receives his first major exposure to literature upon becoming the servant of Miquis, "literato y poeta" (poet and man of letters), who lives in the world of the imagination (1:1394). As Felipe listens to his master, who recites his dramatic work, the words on the page become transformed into reality in the protagonist's eyes:

Cuando llegaba Alejandro a una escena dramática en que había choque de espadas, uno que se cae, otro que grita, o cosa así, ya estaba Felipe con los pelos de punta, lo mismo que si presenciara el lance entre personas de carne y hueso. Pues digo... , si el poeta leía una escena de amor, con ternezas y sentimientos expresados a lo vivo, ya estaba Felipe soltando de sus ojos lagrimones como garbanzos. (1:1396)

(When Alejandro came to a dramatic scene in which there were clashes of swords, with one person falling and another one shouting, or things of that sort, there was Felipe with his hair standing on end, as if he were witnessing a duel between persons of flesh and blood. And... , if the poet read a love scene, with endearments and feelings expressed in a lifelike manner, there was Felipe letting out from his eyes tears as large as chick peas.)

---

ship between the signified and the referent, as in the case of Juanito el Socorro's name, can also be seen as a manifestation of this "hypersemanticity." Although ironic language, on the one hand, calls attention to the arbitrary relationship between the sign and the referent, it can also affirm the power of established conventions by merely reversing this relationship rather than subverting it altogether. Compare Maxi's struggle with the linguistic conventions of society (see Chapter 1 above).

Felipe falls into the trap of illusionist art once again, as he did in the bullfighting episode: he loses a sense of the distance that separates the reader (or spectator) from the work of fiction.

Felipe's vision of literature is diametrically opposed to that of Alejandro Miquis, who perceives it as fiction freed from the referent, whether this referent is nature or the social construct. The playwright's idealism is reminiscent of Maxi Rubín's mystical philosophy, through which Maxi seeks to free language from the world (see Chapter 1 above).[17] On one level, Miquis's play, *El grande Osuna*, is Galdós's parody of the romantic melodrama, a genre that denies the connection between language and reality.[18] The narrator, ironically adopting society's perspective, refers to the character's literary activity as "peligrosísimo ejercicio de la imaginación" (a very dangerous exercise of the imagination; 1:1394). Alejandro models the heroine of his drama, La Carniola, on the object of his desire in real life, the vulgar and opportunistic "La Tal." (The seemingly nondescript name *La Tal* is in itself another example of the motivated sign: it reflects the character's worthlessness and vulgarity.) When Felipe warns his master of his lover's true character, Miquis responds:

Yo me enamoro de lo que yo veo, no de lo que ven los demás; yo purifico con mi entendimiento lo que aparece tachado de impureza . . . Yo voy siempre tras de lo absoluto. Los seres, las acciones, las formas todas las

17. It is also worthy of note that the narrator's description of Miquis in *El doctor Centeno*—"Físicamente era raquítico y de constitución muy pobre, con la fatalidad de ser dado a derrochar sus escasas fuerzas vitales" (Physically, he was rickety and very weak-bodied, with the fatality of being given to waste his scant vital forces; 1:1393)—is similar to the portrayal of Maxi in *Fortunata y Jacinta*: "Maximiliano era raquítico, de naturaleza pobre y linfática, absolutamente privado de gracias personales" (Maximiliano was rickety, weak, lymphatic, and completely devoid of physical charm; 2:592).

18. Gustavo Correa sees in the play's accumulation of adventure and intrigue a manifestation of Miquis's desire to transport himself imaginatively to the anachronistic world of Calderón's honor plays and of his "comedias de capa y de espada": "Alejandro Miquis se identificó con un ideal literario, que en este caso es el específico del mundo artístico de Calderón" (Alejandro Miquis identified with a literary ideal which, in this case, is specific to the artistic world of Calderón) ("Pérez Galdós y la tradición calderoniana," 230). José Luis López Muñoz likewise notes that Miquis seeks the world of the past ("el mundo de la fantasía" [the world of fantasy]) through his dramatic work ("Felipe Centeno," 254).

cojo y, a la fuerza, las llevo hacia aquella meta gloriosa donde está la idea, y las acomodo al canon de la idea misma. (1:1449)

(I fall in love with what I see, not with what others see; I purify in my mind what appears to be faulted with impurity . . . I always go after the absolute. I take beings, actions, forms, and I forcibly take them to that glorious goal where idea is to be found, and I accommodate them to the canon of idea itself.)

Like Maxi, who adores Fortunata at the end of *Fortunata y Jacinta* in "el tálamo incorruptible de mi pensamiento" (the incorruptible nuptial chamber of my thought), Alejandro Miquis transforms the object of his desire through language (2:980). "La Tal," like Don Quixote's Dulcinea and Maxi's Fortunata, becomes a pure ideal. Unlike Maxi, however, Miquis ultimately relinquishes his fiction and comes to terms with the "reality" that is transparent to the others around him. On his deathbed, he confesses his abhorrence for La Carniola—"La Tal"— and his wish to destroy *El grande Osuna*, the child of his imagination.

Although both of Felipe's masters free language from the world and from meaning, Pedro Polo conceals the gap between the signifier and the signified, between the sign and the referent, whereas Alejandro Miquis openly acknowledges this gap through his creative activity. Different as these two characters are, their attitudes toward the sign serve as a contrast to Felipe's vision of language. Their two worlds are linked by the protagonist, who passes through both of them. The first of these, the world of Pedro Polo, exemplifies society as a whole. Felipe's education within the false semiotic system of society is problematic as long as he searches for a true referent behind its signs. Miquis's world, on the other hand, represents a fiction that has renounced its connection to the real world. Felipe, who comes into contact with autonomous language upon entering Miquis's service, does not remain untouched by his master's creative aspirations. For example, he develops a certain consciousness of poetic language: his amateur effort to compose his own poetry is governed by an awareness of what is or is not "palabra de poesía" (a poetic word; 1:1418). In the scene of Miquis's death, it is Felipe, ironically, who protests the destruction of his master's romantic fiction. Nonetheless, his fundamental quest for truth ultimately brings him back to the signified.

The tension between the two conflicting attitudes toward the sign finds expression in the dialogue between Felipe Centeno and José Ido del Sagrario, a writer of serial novels, in the final scene of *El doctor Centeno*. In this scene, the two characters appear to step out of the fictional world to comment upon it as literature. As Ido del Sagrario explains the art of producing serial novels to Felipe, the latter declares:

> ARISTOTELES. (Con inocencia.)—Pues, hombre de Dios, si quiere componer libros para entretener a la gente y hacerla reír y llorar, no tiene más que llamarme; yo le cuento todo lo que nos ha pasado a mi amo y a mí, y conforme yo se lo vaya contando, usted lo va poniendo en escritura. (1:1468)

> (ARISTOTLE. [With innocence.]—Well, man of God, if you want to compose books to entertain people and make them laugh and cry, just call me; I'll tell you everything that's happened to me and my master, and as I tell it to you, you can put it down in writing.)

By envisioning "real life" to be the most suitable material for the novel, Felipe sustains a belief in the mimetic theory of literature: he views it as a faithful reflection of a preexistent reality. Ido, on the other hand, has a different perspective:

> IDO. (Con suficiencia.)—¡Cómo se conoce que eres un chiquillo y no estás fuerte en letras! Las cosas comunes y que están pasando todos los días no tienen el gustoso saborete que es propio de las inventadas, extraídas de la imaginación. La pluma del poeta se ha de mojar en la ambrosía de la mentira hermosa, y no en el caldo de la horrible verdad. (1:1468)

> (IDO. [With self-assurance.]—It's obvious that you're a child and that you aren't strong in letters! Common things that are happening every day don't have the savory taste that's characteristic of invented things, taken from the imagination. The poet's pen should be dipped in the ambrosia of beautiful lies, and not in the broth of horrible truths.)

Ido del Sagrario, unlike Felipe, considers literature to be a fiction that has renounced its connection to the tangible world. Like Miquis, he begins by modeling his work on the "mundo visible" (visible world) but ultimately transforms it into an autonomous fiction freed from the referent (1:1468).[19] Ido brings to mind once more the figure of Maximiliano Rubín in *Fortunata y Jacinta*, who aspires to a state of *Pensamiento puro* in which the soul is freed from the flesh, the individual from society, and language from the world.

It is ironical, of course, that what Felipe considers to be real life is a fiction for the reader of the novel, who has just finished reading the story of Felipe Centeno and his master. It is doubly paradoxical that the imaginative narrative the reader has been following is what Ido regards as "real life" and therefore inappropriate as subject matter for a novel. The irony here, in a typically Galdosian fashion, simultaneously undermines the positions of both characters. Felipe's dialogue with Ido del Sagrario, which takes the form of a theoretical exposition, anticipates the exchange between Segismundo Ballester and the literary critic Ponce in Fortunata's funeral scene in *Fortunata y Jacinta*:

> No toleraba él [Ponce] que la vida se llevase al arte tal como es, sino aderezada, sazonada con olorosas especias y después puesta al fuego hasta que cueza bien. Segismundo no participaba de tal opinión, y estuvieron discutiendo sobre esto con selectas razones de una y otra parte, quedándose cada cual con sus ideas y su convicción, y resultando al fin que la fruta cruda bien madura es cosa muy buena, y que también lo son las compotas, si el repostero sabe lo que trae entre manos. (2:977)

> (He [Ponce] didn't tolerate "raw life" being brought into art, but rather, it had to be dressed and seasoned with aromatic spices and then put on the fire until thoroughly cooked. Segismundo did not share his opinion, and they were arguing this matter, each one advancing his select reasons, but each sticking to his own ideas and convictions, so that in the end they agreed that well-ripened raw fruit was very good, but so were the compotes, if the cook knew what he had in his hands.)

The narrator of the novel maintains an ironic distance from both naive realism and pure aestheticism: he parodies not only Segismundo's inclination to view literature as history, or raw life (suggested by the

19. Once again, the name of the character is significant: *Ido*, the participle of *ir* (to go), suggests a state of absence, and *el sagrario* (sacrarium), a reference to the receptacle for the consecrated elements of the Eucharist, evokes the image of Christ. Both this absence and the spiritual communion of man with God, represented by the Eucharist, symbolize a liberation from the worldly.

metaphor of "la fruta cruda"), but also the contrary tendency of the
critic to define literature as fiction purified of "life" altogether. The
antithetical attitudes embodied in these two characters dramatize, once
again, the struggle between representation and artistic freedom, mimesis and fictional autonomy.

Felipe's effort to overcome the arbitrariness of the sign presupposes a
belief in a truth behind the social construct. The character's trajectory,
as it sets him in conflict with the semiotic systems of Polo and Miquis,
mirrors the novel itself in the process of creating the illusion of reality.
The mimetic project of the realist novel, as well as Felipe's quest for
knowledge, are based on the notion that language can ultimately lead us
to a preexisting reality behind it. Yet Galdós's work, by exposing Felipe's
conception of the natural sign to be a myth, shows that the realist novel
is "process" as well as "product mimesis."[20] *El doctor Centeno* calls attention to its own status as language, as the product of an arbitrary convention. The absence of a referent behind the sign is reflected not only in
Felipe's inability to achieve true knowledge within the social construct,
but also in the semiotic activities of Polo and Miquis, both of whom
manipulate the sign with a consciousness of its arbitrariness. Felipe
Centeno's interpretive journey, as the unifying force of the novel, exposes the tension in the text between two opposing theories of the sign.

20. Hutcheon, *Narcissistic Narrative*, 38–39.

3

The Struggle for Autonomy in *Tristana*

El deseo de libertad sólo lo sienten los que tienen imaginación.

(Only those who have imagination feel the desire for freedom.)

—Montserrat Roig, *La ópera cotidiana*

Tristana, like *Fortunata y Jacinta* and *El doctor Centeno*, lays bare its fictional process principally, though not exclusively, through the interpretive and creative acts of a principal character. In *Tristana*, the protagonist's desire to replace existing reality with autonomous signs of her own invention contrasts paradigmatically with Felipe Centeno's quest for the natural sign. Her trajectory as manipulator and fabricator of signs becomes a metaphor for the making of the novel. Tristana, who begins as a tabula rasa, gains an identity (or various identities) in the text as she awakens to a linguistic and literary consciousness, recreates herself through this knowledge, and finally fades away into the blank page once more as she loses power over her fiction. Transcending her condition as a "person" and a "woman" within the text, she becomes a sign of the semiotic process that is at work in the novel.[1]

A reading of *Tristana* as a reflection on the sign, furthermore, can place the traditional critical response to the novel in a new light. From the time of its first publication, readers of *Tristana* have tried to reconcile, in different ways, the apparent inconsistency between the central position given to the protagonist's feminist consciousness and what they perceive to be the antifeminist ending of the novel. Emilia Pardo Bazán, in one of the first readings of the work, censures Galdós's failure to develop the "asunto interno" (internal subject) originally promised by the novel: "el despertar del entendimiento y la conciencia de una mujer sublevada contra una sociedad que la condena a perpetua infamia y no le abre ningún camino honroso para ganarse la vida" (the awakening of

---

1. Although Noël Valis also raises Tristana's status from "a mere woman" to an objet d'art, she sees the artistic process as a metaphor for the making of human personality rather than the other way around ("Art, Memory, and the Human in Galdós' *Tristana*").

reason and consciousness in a woman stirred up against a society that condemns her to perpetual disgrace and that refuses to open up for her an honorable way of earning a living).[2] Among more recent critics, Emilio Miró, while he considers Galdós to be an advocate of women's freedom, attributes Tristana's failure to "un mal entendido feminismo" (a badly understood feminism) based solely on illusions.[3] According to Edward Friedman, the ironic voice of the narrator, which makes Tristana "a symbol of the need for equality and of the search for social and poetic justice," confirms "Galdós' feminist position" despite appearances to the contrary.[4] Yet another reader goes so far as to attribute the novel's conclusion to Galdós's reading of antifeminist literature.[5] Coming from a different perspective, Roberto Sánchez turns his attention away from the theme of feminism per se toward the problem of feminine psychology: the novel's "disappointment," he suggests, lies not in the inconsistency of its ideology but in the contradictory and therefore inverisimilar nature of the protagonist's "feminism."[6]

Regardless of their critical or ideological positions, all of these critics are (at least implicitly) troubled by Tristana's unstable and ambiguous identity as a woman and a person.[7] As Theodore Sackett notes, Tris-

---

2. "Tristana," in *Obras completas*, 3:1120. Beth Miller shares Pardo Bazán's disappointment, but adds in Galdós's defense: "Galdós no era marcadamente anti-feminista, aunque sí muy comprometido literariamente con el realismo y lo verosímil" (Galdós was not notably antifeminist, although he was very committed to literary realism and verisimilitude) ("Imagen e ideología en *Tristana* de Galdós," 50). For Miller, the novel's conclusion shows that Galdós is primarily concerned with the "realistic" representation of social reality rather than with the propagation of a specific ideology. Others who have focused their attention on the theme of women's liberation in *Tristana*, though from varying critical and ideological positions, are Carlos Feal Deibe, Leon Livingstone, and Ruth Schmidt. Feal Deibe and Schmidt seem to identify Galdós's views with those of Tristana, who rises up against a society oppressive to women (Carlos Feal Deibe, "*Tristana* de Galdós: capítulo en la historia de la liberación femenina"; Ruth A. Schmidt, "Tristana and the Importance of Opportunity"). Livingstone, on the other hand, interprets the novel as a condemnation of the character's act of rebellion, which, according to him, transgresses the "law of nature" ("The Law of Nature and Women's Liberation in *Tristana*," 93).

3. "*Tristana* o la imposibilidad de ser," 521.

4. "'Folly and a Woman': Galdós' Rhetoric of Irony in *Tristana*," 222, 202.

5. Joaquín Casalduero, *Vida y obra de Galdós*, 107.

6. "Galdós' *Tristana*, Anatomy of a 'Disappointment.'"

7. Kay Engler, who approaches the novel from a Jungian perspective, interprets the irresolution of Tristana's identity as a symptom of the "disintegration of self,"

tana, as well as other characters of the novel, create their own and others' "personalities," only to face the destruction of these invented selves.[8] Yet Tristana is not a person, but a fictional character, an artistic construct, and ultimately a sign on the page.[9] Given a more global semiotic perspective, the critic may view the instability of the protagonist's identity (and hence the absence of an unambiguous "feminist" or "antifeminist" ideology behind the text) as a commentary on the nature of language.[10] The novel presents this self-conscious meditation on the sign through Tristana's struggle for autonomy, both as a woman and as a linguistic construct of her own invention.

When the narrator first introduces Tristana, she is without name or identity: he refers to her quite simply as "señorita en el nombre" (mistress of the house, in name; 3:350). Like Fortunata, who initially appears in *Fortunata y Jacinta* as a tabula rasa, artistic raw material to be molded by various other characters, Tristana begins as a blank slate upon which first the narrator and later she herself will forge her artistic

---

which results from the protagonist's inability to "assimilate the Ghostly lover" and to realize her sacred conviction—her struggle for liberation and self-affirmation—in the world ("The Ghostly Lover: The Portrayal of the Animus in *Tristana*," 108). For Valis, however, Tristana's constant "metamorphoses" exemplify Galdós's "conception of human personality which is at once open-ended and disquieting, supremely modern and ultimately elusive" ("Art, Memory, and the Human," 208).

8. In Sackett's words: "[Galdós's] protagonists are not conceived *a priori* as finished entities. They forge their own personalities before our eyes, and we also bear witness to their destruction. They emerge gradually from a mist of legend and conjecture; they create themselves, giving themselves names and providing meaning for those names" ("Creation and Destruction of Personality in *Tristana*: Galdós and Buñuel," 76).

9. Roland Barthes defines the character in semiotic terms as a construct formed by the convergence of semes (the signifieds of connotation) upon one point: "When identical semes traverse the same proper name several times and appear to settle upon it, a character is created" (*S/Z*, 67). Barthes's statement recalls William Gass's idea that "anything which serves as a fixed point in a narrative functions as a character." In the same essay, Gass emphasizes that a literary character is "not a person" and that "nothing whatever that is appropriate to persons can be correctly said of him" ("The Concept of Character in Fiction," 50, 44).

10. Farris Anderson, from another fresh angle, views Tristana's unstable identity as one of the manifestations of "ellipsis," "the basic aesthetic principle that defines *Tristana* and gives it its coherence" ("Ellipsis and Space in *Tristana*," 62). For Anderson, *Tristana*'s decentering impulse, reflected in its spatial organization, is a mark of the novel's modernity.

identity. As the narrator composes Tristana's linguistic portrait in the opening chapter of the novel, the conventionality of his language evokes a literary archetype rather than a "real" woman. Her "blancura casi inverosímil de puro alabastrina" (her almost unlifelike whiteness of pure alabaster), "los negros ojos más notables por lo vivarachos y luminosos que por lo grandes" (her black eyes, more noteworthy for their vivacity and luminosity than for their size), "las cejas increíbles, como indicadas en arco con la punta de finísimo pincel" (her incredible eyebrows, as if traced in an arch with the tip of a very fine artist's brush), "pequeñuela y roja la boquirrita" (her tiny and red mouth), "los dientes, menudos, pedacitos de cuajado cristal" (her minute teeth, fragments of solidified crystal), and "el cabello . . . brillante como torzales de seda" (her hair . . . shining like silk twines), all bring to mind the image of the Renaissance *bello ideal* (ideal beauty), an archetype to which both Tristana and Horacio repeatedly refer in their future epistolary exchange (3:350). The protagonist emerges as a less-than-real figure traced by the "finísimo pincel" of her creator, and her whiteness ("casi inverosímil") contributes to the sense of her "intrinsic unreality" produced by the conventionality of the narrator's language.[11]

The narrator reinforces the character's unreality in the following description:

Pero lo más característico en tan singular criatura era que parecía toda ella un puro armiño y el espíritu de la pulcritud, pues ni aun rebajándose a las más groseras faenas domésticas se manchaba. Sus manos, de una forma perfecta—¡qué manos!—, tenían misteriosa virtud, como su cuerpo y ropa, para poder decir a las capas inferiores del mundo físico: *la vostra miseria non mi tange*. Llevaba en toda su persona la impresión de un aseo intrínseco, elemental, superior y anterior a cualquier contacto de cosa desaseada o impura. (3:350)

(But the most characteristic thing in this singular creature was that all of her seemed to be pure ermine and the spirit of pulchritude, since she never became blemished even when she lowered herself to the most vulgar domestic tasks. Her hands, of a perfect form—what hands!—, had the mysterious virtue, like her body and clothing, of being able to say to the lower layers of the physical world: *your misery does not touch me*. She carried with herself the impression of an intrinsic and elemental cleanliness, superior and anterior to all contact with untidy or impure things.)

11. Sackett, "Creation and Destruction," 75.

He not only calls attention to Tristana's angelic purity, but compares her explicitly to another literary figure—Dante's Beatrice—by placing the latter's words in her mouth. [12] Like Beatrice, who remains untouched by sin and suffering even when sent from Heaven on a mission of mercy to the underworld, Tristana appears to reject the impurity of the tangible world. The narrator's insistence on Tristana's purity and on her other-worldliness is at first ironical, since she is neither sexually innocent (she is Don Lope's concubine) nor removed from the miseries of the physical world. Nevertheless, this description, which anticipates the implicit comparison between Tristana and the whiteness of an unprinted page, calls attention to the fact that the character is no more than a purely fictional entity. The perfect form of her hands, evocative once again of the conventional *bello ideal*, and her intrinsic cleanliness (the adjective *intrinsic* can mean *self-contained*, as in the world of art) also help to produce an aura of unreality. Her likeness to an *image* of a "dama japonesa de alto copete" (Japanese lady with a raised hairpiece; 3:350) is comparable to Máximo Manso's status in *El amigo Manso* as a being twice removed from reality, "sueño de sueño y sombra de sombra" (dream of a dream and shadow of a shadow; 1:1185). Finally, Tristana's paperlike quality, which brings the artist's canvas to the narrator's mind ("toda ella parecía de papel, de ese papel plástico, caliente y vivo en que aquellos inspirados representan lo divino y lo humano" [all of her seemed to be made of paper, of that plastic paper, warm and alive, upon which those inspired artists represent what is divine and human; 3:350]) recalls that she is, in the end, no more than an image conjured up by words on a blank page. The narrator of *Tristana* reveals the protagonist's fictional condition in much the same way as Máximo Manso affirms his nonexistence in the first chapter of *El amigo Manso*. [13]

Only after he completes his portrayal of the "señorita en el nombre" does the narrator mention Tristana by name: "Falta explicar el paren-

12. These words ("la vostra miseria non mi tange") appear in *Inferno*, 2.92. In this passage, Virgil tells Dante how Beatrice came to him in Limbo to send him to rescue the poet from the *selva oscura* by leading him through the whole infernal realm. When Virgil expresses amazement that anyone would leave Paradise to descend into Hell on such a mission, Beatrice responds that God's grace has kept misery from touching her even in this infernal place. I would like to thank Professor Paul Olson, editor of *MLN*, for pointing out this reference.

13. The reference to Tristana as a "linda figurilla de papel" (pretty little paper figure; 3:350) in the second chapter similarly brings to mind the fictional beings of *El amigo Manso*—the "desgraciadas figurillas" (wretched little figures; 1:1310) that their creator must leave behind at the conclusion of the novel.

tesco de Tristana, que por este nombre respondía la mozuela bonita, con el gran don Lope" (The relationship between Tristana—the pretty little lass answered to this name—and the great Don Lope still needs to be explained; 3:350). Significantly, the narrator, rather than giving the protagonist a definitive name that fixes her identity in the text, states that "Tristana" is simply the name to which she responds. The public's conjectures as to her kinship with Don Lope reinforce the sense of her unstable identity, which the apparent contingency of her name generates. According to the narrator, "versiones había para todos los gustos" (there were versions for all tastes): one moment, she is Don Lope's niece; after a few months, she is his daughter or wife; and, finally, "no era hija, ni sobrina, ni esposa, ni nada del gran don Lope; no era nada y lo era todo" (she was neither daughter, nor niece, nor wife, nor anything of the great Don Lope; she was nothing and everything; 3:350). The last words, "no era nada y lo era todo," refer not only to the protagonist's relationship with Lope and to her place in society, but also to her ontological status in the literary work. The narrator affirms Tristana's nonexistence as a fictional being at the same time as he anticipates all of the roles and identities that she will later adopt through her own and others' creative acts. The metaphor of the "muñeca" (mannequin) therefore characterizes her lifelessness in this state of potential fictional realization. Finally, the comparison between Tristana and the "petaca" (chest) at the conclusion of the first chapter is significant: the chest, which evokes the image of an empty container, may be seen as a metaphor for the empty sign that is open to possible meanings.

Tristana, as a sign, becomes the object of creation from the moment in which her mother, Josefina Solís, gives her a name of literary significance. An amateur writer of verse and a devotee of Golden Age drama, the quixotic Josefina names her daughter after Tristan, the hero of medieval legends of chivalry, in an effort to revive a mythical society that, in her eyes, serves as "norma y ejemplo a nuestras realidades groseras y vulgares" (norm and example for our vulgar and common reality; 3:354).[14] Josefina Solís is thus twice Tristana's creator: first, by virtue of her motherhood, and secondly, by the act of naming her daughter. Her literary invention of Tristana is significant in light of the fact that Josefina detests "las modernas tendencias realistas" (modern

14. Germán Gullón examines the parallels between Galdós's novel and the myth of Tristan and Isolde (*"Tristana,"* 17). For a summary of the different versions of this legend, see Margaret Drabble, ed., *The Oxford Companion to English Literature*, 998–99.

realist tendencies) in literature and worships "el ideal y la frase noble y decorosa" (the ideal, and the noble and dignified style; 3:353). With age, she forgets the fictional world that has formed a major part of her existence and withdraws instead into her manias, which can be seen as an extension of her quixotism. Her "manía de mudarse de casa" (mania of moving), which the narrator attributes to her "ansia infinita de lo desconocido" (limitless longing for the unknown), represents her constant search for an ideal world that exists only in the imagination (3:353). Her compulsive cleanliness, similarly, becomes a symbolic act through which she aspires to a purified reality. Finally, Josefina, like "Don Quijote moribundo" (the dying Don Quixote), leaves the world by renouncing the fictions of her past (3:354).

The equally quixotic Don Lope, to whom Josefina entrusts her daughter on her deathbed, takes upon himself the role of Tristana's "parent" and shaper after her mother's death. The narrator highlights Lope's likeness to Cervantes's hero from the very first page of the novel. He introduces Lope by echoing the opening lines of *Don Quixote*: "En el populoso barrio de Chamberí, más cerca del Depósito de aguas que de Cuatro Caminos, vivía no ha muchos años un hidalgo de buena estampa y nombre peregrino" (In the populous district of Chamberí, closer to the Reservoir than to Cuatro Caminos, there lived not so long ago a nobleman with a pleasant countenance and an odd name; 3:349). In the subsequent lines, the narrator of *Tristana*, not unlike the playful "first author" of Cervantes's novel, brings the reader's attention to the problem of Don Lope's various names. According to the narrator, some of Lope's friends call him *don Lope de Sosa*, a name that reveals the literary nature of the character's existence.[15] Don Lope, like Alonso Quijano, recreates himself through the imitation of literary models, among which are the chivalric romance, the Calderonian honor play, and the Don Juan archetype.[16] The ironic narrator, by constantly calling attention to

15. Lope de Sosa is a figure who appears in "Cena jocosa," one of the festive poems of the late-Renaissance poet Baltasar de Alcázar. The speaker of the poem, who begins with an allusion to Lope de Sosa, never completes the story that he sets out to narrate.

16. For other discussions of Lope's self-inventive act, see Francisco Ayala, "Galdós entre el lector y los personajes," 8; Kronik, "*El amigo Manso* and the Game of Fictive Autonomy," 74; and especially David Goldin, "Calderón, Cervantes, and Irony in *Tristana*," 100–101. Goldin demonstrates how the characters' self-creative acts produce the multiple ironic perspectives through which the novel questions anachronistic literary and social codes.

Lope's fictions, exposes them to ridicule: for example, he refers to Lope as "el Don Juan en decadencia" (a decadent Don Juan; 3:373), mockingly compares his appearance to the "varonil y avellanada hermosura de cuadro de *Las Lanzas*" (dark and virile beauty of the painting of *Las Lanzas*; 3:375), ironically praises the character's "sistema seudocaballeresco" (pseudo-chivalric system; 3:352), and, on one occasion, responds to Lope's words to Tristana with the exclamation, "¡Lástima que no hablara en verso para ser perfecta imagen del *padre noble* de antigua comedia!" (What a shame that he wasn't speaking in verse so that he could be the perfect image of the *noble father* in the old-style plays!; 3:374). Lope himself is aware of his self-fictionalization, as he reveals in his declaration to Tristana: "No quiero hacer el celoso de comedia" (I don't want to play the part of the jealous man in the *comedia*; 3:374).

The act of (re)naming represents the first step in Lope's literary self-transformation. The narrator declares: "pero él respondía por don Lope Garrido. Andando el tiempo, supe que la partida de bautismo rezaba *don Juan López Garrido*, resultando que aquel sonoro *don Lope* era composición del caballero" (but he went by Lope Garrido. With the passage of time, I found out that his baptismal certificate read *don Juan López Garrido*, and it turned out that the sonorous *don Lope* was the gentleman's invention; 3:349).[17] The narrator lays bare the artificial nature of Lope's name, but this name, in the narrator's vision, actually corresponds to Garrido's personal characteristics: "y tan bien caía [este nombre] en su cara enjuta, de líneas firmes y nobles, tan buen acomodo hacía el nombre con la espigada tiesura del cuerpo, con la nariz de caballete . . . que el sujeto no se podía llamar de otra manera" (it was so well-suited to his lean face, marked by firm and noble lines; the name went so well with the slender stiffness of his body and with his high-bridged nose . . . that the subject could not be called by any other name; 3:349). The correspondence between the name and the character behind it, together with the sonorous quality of Lope's name (which in itself suggests a relation of imitation between the signifier and the sig-

17. William Gass claims that proper names have always held a special excitement for the writer because their meanings, unlike those of other words that he or she uses, have not yet been formed. For the writer, the creation of character represents the opportunity to "give fresh meaning to new words" ("The Concept of Character in Fiction," 51).

nified), reveal, once again, the "Cratylean consciousness of signs," which, according to Barthes, underlies all acts of "poetic" creation.[18]

As in the case of Gabriel de Araceli (in the first series of the *Episodios nacionales*), Lope's self-transformation is directly related to his ability to manipulate the word. The narrator calls attention to the "arte sutilísimo de la palabra y finezas galantes de superior temple" (most subtle art of the word and fine gallantries of the utmost audacity; 3:356) with which Lope carries out his tyrannical seduction of women and to the authority that language gives him within his household: "sabía hermanar las palabras atentas y familiares con la autoridad de amo indiscutible" (he knew how to join polite and familiar words with the indisputable authority of the head of the household; 3:350). At first, Lope's linguistic authority relegates Tristana to her role as the object of his creative activity—as an object to whom a voice is denied. Yet it is Lope who, as her teacher, stirs up her imagination ("la fácil disposición de la joven para idealizar las cosas, para verlo todo como no es, o como nos conviene o nos gusta que sea" [the ready inclination of the young girl to idealize things, to see everything not as it is, but as it suits us, or as we would like it to be; 3:356]) and awakens her to a consciousness of language ("[Tristana] aprendió también a disimular, a valerse de las ductilidades de la palabra" [she also learned how to feign, to make use of the ductility of the word; 3:357]) that will soon transform her into a creator figure in her own right.[19] The narrator, reflecting upon Tris-

18. *New Critical Essays*, 55–68. Compare the names "El doctor Centeno" and "Miss Fly." Don Quixote's (re)creation of Rocinante, "nombre, a su parecer, alto, sonoro y significativo" (to his thinking, a lofty, sonorous and meaningful name), similarly presupposes a belief in the motivation of the sign (Cervantes, *Don Quijote*, 1:76). Galdós's echoing of Cervantes's word *sonoro* cannot be dismissed as coincidental.

19. Clarín has interpreted *Tristana* as "la representación bella de un *destino gris* atormentando un alma noble, bella, pero débil, de verdadera fuerza sólo para imaginar, para soñar, de muchas actitudes embrionarias, un alma como hay muchas en nuestro tiempo de medianías llenas de ideal y sin energía ni vocación seria, constante, definida" (the beautiful representation of a gray destiny tormenting a noble soul, beautiful but weak, with a true strength only to imagine, to dream; a soul with many infantile attitudes, a kind of soul that is common in these times of mediocrity, full of ideals and energy without a serious, constant, and defined vocation) (*Galdós*, 252). The author of *La Regenta* sees Tristana as a reflection of his own heroine, Ana Ozores, who transforms reality according to her knowledge of the imaginary world of romantic literature. In the process of her creative awakening, Tristana imagines

tana's linguistic and moral apprenticeship with Lope, properly identifies the relationship between the two characters as that of "discípula" (disciple) and "maestro" (master; 3:357).

Tristana's linguistic awakening corresponds to the emergence of her feminist identity. When the protagonist finally speaks in her own voice after four chapters of silence, she affirms, to Lope's servant Saturna, her newly gained belief in women's liberation. She asserts her convictions, not through action, but through speech, by pronouncing the word *libertad* (freedom), whose meaning women have long been denied. (Saturna responds: "Libertad, tiene razón la señorita; libertad, aunque esta palabra no suena bien en boca de mujeres" [Freedom, you're right, young lady; freedom, although this word does not sound good in a woman's mouth; 3:357], thus calling attention to its condition as word.) In the same conversation, Tristana invents language (the feminine "médicas" [doctors], "abogadas" [lawyers], "boticarias" [pharmacists], "escribanas" [clerks], etc., forms that we can assume were not in usage in the nineteenth century) in an effort to engender new realities for women. Her aspiration to become a writer and to study foreign tongues reveals her awareness of the possibilities of language and anticipates her subsequent creative acts.

Tristana's imaginative inclinations take on new meaning with the appearance of Horacio Díaz. The painter, who emerges unexpectedly one day from among the *sordomudos* (deaf-mutes), becomes the object of her fictionalizations. By transforming a woman into a creator figure, *Tristana* reverses the traditional pattern—of the male author and the female text—that tends to dominate many literary works. When her obsession with Horacio begins, Tristana knows no more about him than what she glimpses from a distance: a man without name, voice, or identity, he disappears from sight as soon as he appears, leaving nothing but an image in her mind. Significantly, the narrator recounts the scene of the lovers' first meeting not from the viewpoint of an omniscient and detached observer, but from the protagonist's perspective. He refers repeatedly to Horacio (still without name) as "el desconocido" (the

---

"dramas de los que hacen llorar y piezas de las que hacen reír, y novelas de muchísimo enredo y pasiones tremendas" (the kind of drama that makes one cry and plays that make one laugh, and novels with a lot of intrigue and great passions; 3:358), imitations of "romantic" literature that are often parodied in realist works. Both Tristana and Ana exemplify, in some ways, the heroine of what Harry Levin has called the literature of "systematic disillusionment" (*The Gates of Horn*, 48).

stranger) or "el caballero incógnito" (the unknown gentleman), as if the narrator, too, were living Tristana's experience. As a result, the reader is obliged to share the vision of the protagonist, who has no prior knowledge of Horacio's life or history. When the narrator asks, "¿Qué hombre era aquél?" (Who was that man?; 3:362), he simultaneously echoes Tristana's thoughts and anticipates the question of the reader, who sees this man as a blank slate upon which a story is about to be written. Horacio's entrance into the text thus virtually mirrors Tristana's birth as an artistic construct in the first chapter of the novel. Immediately before her initial encounter with her future lover, Tristana comes into contact with a group of blind and deaf-mute children who symbolize her condition. She identifies especially with the mute youngsters, who are deprived of language and must invent an alternative system of signs ("gestos, muecas, cucamonas mil" [gesticulations, grimaces, wheedling a thousandfold; 3:361]) in order to communicate among themselves. Similarly, the protagonist fabricates a fictional world that stands apart from society, because this society denies her (and all women) the right to speak.

Horacio emerges in the novel as a metaphorical canvas upon which the protagonist projects her fiction of the ideal lover—a fiction that she has invented prior to the painter's actual appearance. She is therefore able to love the "caballero incógnito" even before she meets him. Tristana's idealization of a man yet unknown to her brings to mind Maxi Rubín's struggle to reconcile the "real" woman, Fortunata, with the ideal construct of the "mujer honrada" that exists prior to his acquaintance with any woman. Significantly, when Tristana and Horacio break their silence for the first time, the narrator exclaims: "¿Qué dijo a Tristana el sujeto aquel? No se sabe. Sólo consta que Tristana le contestó a todo que sí, ¡sí, sí!" (What did that subject say to Tristana? We don't know. All that's clear is that Tristana answered him yes, yes, yes, to everything; 3:363). The narrator's sudden shift from a position of omniscience to the role of a limited observer undercuts the credibility of his professed lack of knowledge. He withholds the words of Horacio (to whom he refers as "el sujeto aquel") in order to focus attention on the protagonist's verbal affirmation, the triple use of "sí" that marks the origin of her role as Horacio's creator.

After their first encounter, the lovers communicate to each other through writing, and only after Tristana has already written a number of letters to Horacio do the two meet face to face again. In recounting the characters' second meeting, the narrator reveals the protagonist's surprise upon finding that her lover appears significantly younger than she has initially imagined. Although the question of Horacio's age is in itself insignificant, the narrator, by calling attention to the protagonist's disillusionment, suggests her tendency to fictionalize the object of her desire.[20] In her third letter, she writes:

> Te estoy queriendo, te estoy buscando desde antes de nacer . . . No formes mala idea de mí si me presento a ti sin ningún velo, pues el del falso decoro con que el mundo ordena que se encapuchen nuestros sentimientos se me deshizo entre las manos cuando quise ponérmelo. Quiéreme como soy. (3:363)

> (I have been loving you, I have been looking for you since before my birth . . . Don't form a bad impression of me if I present myself to you without a veil, because that of false decorum with which the world orders us to cover up our feelings dissolved in my hands when I tried to put it on. Love me as I am.)

Although she claims to present herself without any masks, her letters are mediated by conventional language. The very notion of a true self, freed from the "falso decoro" of society, is a product of the romantic imagination. Tristana, by rejecting social convention, believes that she is identifying herself with nature, yet in reality she is merely replacing one convention with another that is equally arbitrary. Her romanticism leads her to imagine that "el hombre que le había deparado el Cielo era una excepción entre todos los mortales" (the man whom Heaven had granted her was an exception among all mortals; 3:366). For Tristana, love comes to represent a mystical experience through which she seeks a state of perfect communion with the man whom she has transformed into a divine figure; yet, in her perpetual search for the "más allá," she is never able to attain this ideal.

20. Jennifer Lowe, who examines the significance of the theme of age in *Tristana*, writes: "The difficulty of making firm assessments of an individual's age is clearly exemplified and, indeed, is just one aspect of the wider issue of the unreliability of human judgments and the significant effects of delusion demonstrated in this novel" ("Age, Illusion and Irony in *Tristana*," 109). The entire notion of "reliability," however, becomes problematic once we begin to see all reality in the text as a product of the imagination.

Horacio, in turn, participates in Tristana's fiction by adopting conventional roles and by imitating the language of romanticism:

Nuestro romanticismo, nuestra exaltación, no nos parecieron absurdos. Nos sorprendimos con hambre atrasada, el hambre espiritual, noble y pura que mueve el mundo, y por la cual existimos, y existirán miles de generaciones después de nosotros. (3:368)

(Our romanticism, our exaltation, didn't seem absurd to us. We surprised ourselves with a delayed hunger, a spiritual, noble and pure hunger that moves the world, and for which we exist and thousands of generations after us will exist.)

Horacio's "spiritualism," as the narrator calls it, is somewhat analogous to the protagonist's "mystical" quest. At the same time, the ideal woman that Horacio invents is not solely the result of a literary convention, but also a product of the laws of patriarchal society: "había soñado en Tristana la mujer subordinada al hombre en inteligencia y en voluntad, la esposa que vive de la savia moral e intelectual del esposo y que con los ojos y con el corazón de él ve y siente" (he had dreamed of Tristana as a woman subordinate to man in intelligence and in will, the wife who subsists on the moral and intellectual sap of the husband and who sees and feels with his eyes and his heart; 3:377).[21] The painter's ideal woman therefore becomes increasingly removed from the feminist self-identity that Tristana has constructed through language. She, however, ironically continues to love the ideal Horacio even as she affirms her desire for independence. Her defense of feminist principles is directly related to her creative role: she seeks to impose her own text on the male subject, rather than conforming to the role of the woman as the text to be written. She symbolically asserts her power as originator by insisting, to Horacio's dismay, that their child (not yet conceived) bear her last name.

Soon after the beginning of their secret rendezvous, Horacio refines Tristana's linguistic skill by immersing her in the world of literature:

21. As one critic has noted, Horacio's unwillingness to abandon the real world completely is symbolized by his commonplace surname (Emilio Miró, "*Tristana* o la imposibilidad de ser," 512). The ordinary *Díaz* stands in ironic juxtaposition to his first name, which evokes the figure of a poet.

Casi sin proponérselo, [Horacio] dio a su amiguita lecciones del *bel parlare*. Con su asimilación prodigiosa, Tristana dominó en breves días la pronunciación, y leyendo a ratos como por juego, y oyéndole leer a él, a las dos semanas recitaba con admirable entonación de actriz consumada el pasaje de Francesca, el de Ugolino y otros. (3:382)

(Almost without trying, he [Horacio] gave his friend lessons in *bel parlare*. With her prodigious assimilation, Tristana mastered pronunciation in a short time, and reading from time to time as if it were a game and hearing him read, she was reciting, after two weeks, the passage about Francesca, Ugolino, and others with the admirable intonation of a consummate actress.)

Their knowledge of various linguistic and literary conventions allows them to invent a private lovers' vocabulary, through which they recreate themselves and each other.[22] As Germán Gullón has shown, the characters transport themselves onto "el plano de la literaturización" (the plane of literaturization) by reinventing their identity according to literary archetypes.[23] Tristana no longer responds to her original name, but to "Beatrice," "Francesca," and "la Paca de Rímini"; Horacio, modeled on the Tenorio archetype, becomes "señó Juan." Finally, the lovers transform don Lope into the figure of the villain, the "tirano de Siracusa" (tyrant of Syracuse), whose amorous intrigues, according to Tristana's literary vision, are "todas muy novelescas" (all very novelesque; 3:383). Significantly, the episode of Paolo and Francesca, the text alluded to within Galdós's text, self-consciously mirrors the outer text: Horacio and Tristana model themselves on Dante's Paolo and Francesca, who, in turn, live in imitation of the legendary Lancelot and Guinevere.[24] The (self-)transformative act of Tristana and her lover

22. See Sobejano for an analysis of the "vocabulario de los amantes" (vocabulary of the lovers) and of its function within Galdós's dialogic art ("Galdós y el vocabulario de los amantes").

23. "*Tristana*: literaturización y estructura novelesca," 25.

24. In the *Inferno*, Francesca tells the pilgrim Dante that the reading of literature has inspired her love affair with Paolo: "We read one day for pastime of Lancelot, how love constrained him. We were alone and had no misgiving. Many times that reading drew our eyes together and changed the colour in our faces, but one point alone it was that mastered us; when we read that the longed-for smile was kissed by so great a lover, he who never shall be parted from me, all trembling, kissed my mouth. A Galeotto was the book and he that wrote it" (Dante, *Inferno*, 79).

reminds us, once again, that the character is nothing more than a tissue of texts and, as such, can have no existence outside language.

Horacio's departure and the beginning of the lovers' epistolary exchange marks a turning point in Tristana's literary endeavor. The ironic narrator, who until this moment has repeatedly exposed the characters' textuality, fades into the background as the two begin to speak directly through their letters. Tristana's voice, in particular, gains a central place in the narration as her letters come to occupy a greater proportion of textual space. The protagonist's growing presence corresponds to her increasing power over the sign. Horacio's absence represents the removal of the referent that ties her fiction to the real world: as a result, she is able to invent freely, to fill the empty sign with a *fictional* referent.

In the first letters following the lovers' separation, Tristana struggles to reconcile *her* Horacio, a fictional being, with the Horacio that she suspects may exist in the real world. She writes in one letter:

Dime: ¿existes tú, o no eres más que un fantasma vano, obra de la fiebre, de esta ilusión de lo hermoso y de lo grande que me trastorna? Hazme el favor de echar para acá una carta *fuera de abono*, o un telegrama que diga: *Existo. Firmado, señó Juan*. (3:387)

(Tell me, do you exist, or are you no more than an empty phantasm, a product of fever, of this illusion of beauty and greatness, which bewilders me? Do me the favor of sending me a letter with no strings attached, or a telegram that says: *I exist. Signed, señó Juan*.)

Tristana's question "¿existes tú?" is naturally ironic, since the man that she addresses in her letters exists only as language. She can therefore ask for nothing more than the written word (*existo*) as a proof of her correspondent's existence.

In her subsequent letters, Tristana gradually removes her ideal lover from all connection with the referent, the "true" Horacio, although his absence continues to preoccupy her. In one of her missives, she affirms: "Lo más raro de cuanto me pasa es que se me ha borrado tu imagen: no veo claro tu lindo rostro; lo veo así como envuelto en una niebla, y no puedo precisar las facciones, ni hacerme cargo de la expresión, de la mirada" (The strangest thing that's happening to me is that your image has become obliterated: I don't clearly see your beautiful face; I see it as if it were enveloped in a mist, and I can't specify your features, nor can I

grasp your expression, your gaze; 3:392). Tristana's assertion suggests
that she has never conceived of Horacio as anything other than an
image, as a representation. Now even this image fades away, giving way
to a pure ideal: "Te me vuelves espíritu puro, un ser intangible, un... no
sé cómo decirlo. Cuando considero la pobreza de palabras, me dan
ganas de inventar muchas, a fin de que todo pueda decirse" (You're
becoming pure spirit, an intangible being, a... I don't know how to say
it. When I consider the poverty of words, I feel like inventing many
more so that everything can be said; 3:392). The process of romantic
idealization, which parallels the mystical experience, leads to the paradox of the insufficiency of language: the universal ideal (the transcendental "todo") that language is unable to capture is in itself a linguistic
construct, a necessary fiction for the writer to spur on further fabrications.[25] In short, language begets the ineffable, a consciousness of
which, in turn, stimulates the invention of language. In her next letter,
Tristana openly acknowledges that Horacio has become pure invention:

> Me mortifica horriblemente esto de haber perdido la memoria de tu
> carátula. Me paso largos ratos de la noche figurándome cómo eres, sin
> poder conseguirlo. ¿Y qué hace la niña? Reconstruirte a su manera,
> crearte, con violencias de la imaginación. (3:393)

> (Having lost the memory of your mask mortifies me horribly. I spend a

25. Jorge Guillén, in *Lenguaje y poesía*, views the ineffability topos as the common
ground for mystical and romantic literature (75–141): "El poeta místico no puede
expresar lo que sabe, sufre y goza, y en las palabras no encontrará sino soluciones
insuficientes. Hasta partiendo de una vida interior sin fondo sobrenatural, el poeta
profano tampoco logrará transmitir con palabras adecuadas visiones y emociones.
Ante el 'soñador' del siglo XIX vuelve a plantearse el problema de la expresión en
condiciones análogas a las del místico" (The mystic poet cannot express what he
knows, suffers, and takes pleasure in, and he will find only insufficient solutions in
words. Neither will the secular poet, though he starts from an interior life without a
supernatural basis, succeed in transmitting visions and emotions with adequate
words. In the presence of the nineteenth-century "dreamer," the problem of expression will be raised once again under conditions analogous to those of the mystic;
113). Tristana, as a creator figure within Galdós's novel, represents one such romantic "soñador." The notion of the insufficiency of language recurs in many of Galdós's
other works. Compare with Federico Viera's words upon his encounter with Orozco's Shadow in *La incógnita* (see Chapter 4 below) and the narrator's portrayal of
Amaranta in *La corte de Carlos IV* (see Chapter 5 below).

lot of time at night imagining what you are like, without success. And what does the girl do? Reconstruct you in her own way, create you, with violent acts of the imagination.)

Through the metaphor of the "carátula," Tristana once again calls attention to the distance that separates her from the "real" Horacio. Not only does she originally experience her lover as a mask constructed through language, but this mask also becomes a memory that is forever lost to her. Tristana's self-conscious affirmation of Horacio's fictionality corresponds to the moment of her maximum presence as a voice in the text. The number of Horacio's letters gradually diminishes, until Tristana becomes the sole narrator of the novel in Chapter 19. Even the third-person narrator, who has previously interspersed editorial comments (such as "Nota del colector" [Compiler's note], "De él a ella" [From him to her], and "De Tristana a Horacio" [From Tristana to Horacio]) in transcribing the lovers' epistles, disappears completely as an explicit presence and yields the word to the protagonist.

Tristana's increasing autonomy as a narrator who rewrites her own identity is closely linked to her struggle for independence as a woman. As she gains control over language, she protests louder than ever before against men's subjugation of women and asserts the woman's right to freedom. Yet her feminist convictions are often expressed through romantic clichés that call attention to themselves through their conventionality. She writes, for example: "una idea mariposeaba en torno de mí, hasta que se me metió en la mollera y allí se quedó; y hecho su nido, ya me tienes con mi plaga de ideítas que me están atormentando" (an idea was flitting about me, until it got into my head and stayed there; and having made its nest, here I am with my plague of little ideas that are tormenting me; 3:393). Tristana's feminist identity is thus another composition of language, and any notion of the true self that she may hold is a myth. Her tendency to speak of herself in the third person (as "la niña," "tu Beatrice," etc.) reminds us that the self exists only as a fictional other.

Tristana's self-realization as a feminist is virtually inseparable from the act of linguistic mastery, because this self is given to her through language. She gains a sense of intellectual identity as she dedicates herself to the study of the English language. Furthermore, Tristana's contact with the female instructor leads her to reflect upon the relationship between language and gender: "[Lope] me ha puesto profesor de inglés, digo, profesora, aunque más bien la creerías del género masculino o del neutro" ([Lope] has gotten me an English teacher, I mean, a woman teacher, although you'd probably think of her in the masculine or the neutral gender), she writes to Horacio, and in the same letter she refers to this teacher as a "*sacerdota protestana*" (Protestant clergywoman; 3:389). Significantly, she concludes this letter with two well-known lines from Shakespeare's plays: "*To be or not to be... All the world* [*sic*] *a stage*" (3:390). Hamlet's words symbolize the protagonist's state of irresolution between self-affirmation and self-denial (as a woman), between existence and nonexistence (as a character). "All the world's a stage" expresses her view of the world as a stage upon which she acts out her fictions. It is therefore not surprising that, in another letter, she explicitly reveals her attraction to the theatrical profession: "Te juro que en este instante me encuentro con alientos para representar los más difíciles dramas de pasión, las más delicadas comedias de gracia y coquetería" (I swear to you that, right now, I find myself with the courage to represent the most difficult dramas of passion, the most delicate plays of wit and charm; 3:393). The representation of fictional roles in the theater is, of course, not unlike Tristana's acts of self-dramatization on the stage of "life."

After Tristana reaches the height of her linguistic power, the novel depicts the gradual dissolution of her fictions, a process that parallels the fading of her voice. The omniscient narrator begins to take over the narration once again, as he intrudes a number of times to comment on the text of her letters. Many of them now dramatize the protagonist's struggle against the referent—the "real" Horacio—that threatens to destroy the ideal that she has fabricated. In an effort to preserve her fiction, she entreats her lover:

> No te opongas a mi deseo, no desvanezcas mi ilusión . . . No me niegues que eres como te sueño. Déjame a mí que te fabrique... ; no, no es ésa la palabra: que te componga... ; tampoco... : que te reconstruya... ; tampoco... Déjame que te piense conforme a mi real gana. (3:398)

> (Don't stand in the way of my desire, don't make my illusion disappear . . . Don't deny that you are as I dream you. Let me fabricate you... ; no, that isn't the word; compose you... ; that's not it either... ; reconstruct you... ; no... Let me imagine you according to my whim.)

In this highly self-conscious passage, Tristana searches not for a language that captures reality, but for a metalanguage that describes the process by which she invents reality. By thus transporting herself onto a metalinguistic plane, she sets herself at twice remove from the referential world. Her letters, correspondingly, acquire an increasingly solipsistic tone, as if she were speaking to her own imagination rather than to another being outside herself. Tristana's words to Horacio, "soy tu espejo" (I am your mirror; 3:398), suggest that her (by this time imaginary) lover exists not as an independent identity, but only as an agent of her self-creation. The narrator himself affirms that Tristana's letters have no other destination than her imagination: "sólo por mecánica costumbre eran dirigidas a Villajoyosa, pues en realidad debían expedirse por la estafeta de ensueño hacia la estación de los espacios imaginarios" (they were directed to Villajoyosa only through the force of habit, since in reality they should have been dispatched by the courier of daydreams to the station of imaginary spaces; 3:399). Paradoxically, although the protagonist rejects the concrete referent, she is unable to escape from the idea of referentiality altogether. After having struggled to free her fiction from the world, she comes to believe that her creation (the signified) does indeed correspond to the real Horacio (the referent): "Segura estoy de que eres tal y como te pienso" (I'm sure that you're just as I imagine you to be), she writes in one of her epistles (3:398–99).

Although at first Horacio participates willingly in Tristana's fiction, he gradually discovers the distance that separates him from it. Her language, he declares, has no connection with reality: "No me satisface, no, tenerte aquí en espíritu. ¡En espíritu! Retóricas, hija, que llenan los labios y dejan vacío el corazón" (Having you here in spirit doesn't satisfy me, no. In spirit! Rhetoric, child, rhetoric that fills the lips and leaves the heart empty; 3:388). Horacio, in contrast to Tristana, seeks not to exist in a world of autonomous signifiers, but to bring his language back to the referent by escaping into nature. Yet his "nature," which evokes the Renaissance myth of the pastoral, is no closer to reality than is Tristana's idealist fiction. The painter transforms nature into "poesía" (poetry; 3:388) through the use of highly stylized and, at times, baroque literary language. Tristana, by inventing a word (*rustiquidad* [rustiquity; 3:389]) to characterize her lover's life in Villajoyosa, calls attention to the artificiality of his rustic existence. Moreover, his own work of art mediates and makes possible the painter's experience of nature:

El Arte se confabuló con la Naturaleza para conquistarle, y habiendo
pintado un día, después de mil tentativas infructuosas, una marina
soberbia, quedó para siempre prendado del mar azul, de las playas
luminosas y del risueño contorno de tierra. (3:388)

(Art schemed with Nature to conquer him, and having painted a mag-
nificent seascape one day after a thousand unfruitful attempts, he was
forever captivated by the blue sea, the luminous beaches, and the pleasant contour of the earth.)

Horacio's pastoral world is thus another fiction that rivals Tristana's
own. His effort to impose his text upon her, however, is frustrated by the
power of her language, which continues to transform him. As he finds
himself at odds with her fiction, he even begins to doubt his identity:

Vióse convertido en ser ideal, y a cada carta que recibía entrábanle
dudas acerca de su propia personalidad, llegando al extremo increíble
de preguntarse si era él como era, o como lo pintaba con su indómita
pluma la visionaria niña de *don Lepe*. (3:400)

(He saw himself transformed into an ideal, and with each letter that he
received he began to have doubts about his own personality, reaching the
unbelievable extreme of asking himself if he was as he really was, or as
the visionary child of *don Lepe* painted him with her indomitable pen.)

Tristana must ultimately face the gap that separates her fiction from
the referent in the world. By the time she receives news of the operation
that will permanently disfigure her, she has already lost faith in her
ability to beget reality through language. At this point, she becomes
virtually silenced as a voice in the text. She writes only two more letters
to Horacio, both of which are brief and perfunctory. Her penultimate
letter, which she composes with great difficulty, reflects the literal fading
away of her words from the page: "Las últimas líneas apenas se enten-
dían, por el temblor de la escritura. Al soltar la pluma, cayó la muñeca
infeliz en grande abatimiento" (The last lines could scarcely be understood, due to the quivering in her writing. As she let go of her pen, the
unhappy mannequin fell into a state of deep dejection; 3:403). She soon
finds herself physically unable to write and must seek Lope's assistance

in penning her last letter to Horacio. With the loss of the word, the feminist identity that she has constructed also disintegrates.[26]

The letter that Tristana writes to her lover immediately before the amputation of her leg dramatizes her final struggle with referentiality. During some moments, she strives to close the gap between her linguistic creation and the "real" man; during others, she recognizes the autonomy of her language. Only the actual loss of her leg forces her to come to terms with the impossibility of ever reconciling her fiction with the referential world. Her dismemberment comes to represent the final separation between fiction and reality, between the sign and the referent. A change in attitude toward her own painting accompanies Tristana's loss of power over language. Only moments before her amputation, she makes one final effort to preserve her artistic authority by affirming that her painting has become life: "¡Cómo huelen las flores que he pintado! Pero si las pinté creyendo pintarlas, ¿cómo es que ahora me resultan vivas... , vivas? ¡Poder del genio artístico!" (How do the flowers that I've painted smell! But if I painted them believing that I was painting them, how can it be that now they seem alive to me... , alive? Power of artistic genius!; 3:404–5). After her dismemberment, however, Tristana appears to have lost all hope of bringing nature to life through her art. Rather than modeling her paintings on nature, she now prefers to "adestrar la mano en alguna copia" (train her hand with some copy; 3:407). Her art becomes twice removed from reality.

Significantly, the narrator presents Tristana's operation as a moment of symbolic death from which she awakens to a new life. As soon as the character detaches her fiction from the real world, the identity that she has forged meets its death. Yet, the end of her creative process paradox-

26. The failure of Tristana's language raises many questions for the feminist reader. Can an authentically "feminine" language exist within the structure of patriarchal society? Should a "separate but equal" language for women be created at all? These issues have been much debated by feminist critics (Alicia Ostriker, "The Thieves of Language: Women Poets and Revisionist Mythmaking," 315). Applying these questions to Galdós's text, does Tristana's failure as creator suggest that the implied author is somehow censuring the character's rejection of society's (patriarchal) language? Or is he simply affirming the futility of the woman's search for autonomy through language? Still yet, is he condemning Tristana's failure to find a feminine/feminist language that is truly her own? Once again, I believe that Galdós's novel, in its characteristic elusiveness, resists any attempt to find an unambiguous answer to these questions.

ically corresponds to her birth into the text as a completed fictional character. Her exit from the world of referentiality self-consciously mirrors her status as a construct of the imagination. The idea of her "resurrección" (resurrection; 3:405) also establishes a comparison between Tristana and the figure of Christ, who stands at one remove from human society, and brings the reader back full circle to the scene of her first appearance, in which the narrator describes her separation from the physical world. Her martyrlike indifference to physical pain suggests that she has become pure spirit, immune to the enslavement of the body.[27] In the final stages of Tristana's struggle against referentiality, the narrator calls attention to her "mejillas de papel" (paper cheeks; 3:402). Soon after the operation, the protagonist herself notices her paperlike quality: "¿Qué color es este que tengo?" (What kind of complexion do I have?), she exclaims to Saturna; "Parece de papel de estraza" (I seem to have the complexion of rag paper; 3:407). Tristana appears to return to paper, to a state of nonexistence from which she has originally emerged.

By the time Tristana receives notice that Horacio is in Madrid once again, she has almost completely resigned herself to the impossibility of fulfilling her desire in the world. Her wish to escape into the autonomous realm of pure fiction falters only momentarily as she awaits her reunion with Horacio. The imminent reappearance of the real man poses a threat to her ideal lover, since this ideal—a construct of language—is predicated upon absence. When Horacio does actually arrive, Tristana notes the lack of a connection between her fiction and its referent. She is surprised to encounter a stranger whose voice she does not recall (3:411). Like Maximiliano Rubín after Fortunata's death, Tristana detaches her fiction from the world altogether rather than mourning the loss of her ideal:

El ser hermoso y perfecto que amó, construyéndolo ella misma con

---

27. In *El amigo Manso*, the narrator-protagonist similarly finds an end to his suffering as he returns to the realm of pure fiction at the end of the novel: "Al deslizarme de entre sus dedos, envuelto en llamarada roja, el sosiego me dio a entender que había dejado de ser hombre" (As I slipped from between his fingers, enveloped in a red flame, the serenity I felt made me realize that I was no longer a man; 1:1308). During a parallel moment at the beginning of the work when Manso first emerges from the blank page, he asserts: "El dolor me dijo que yo era un hombre" (The pain I felt told me I was a man; 1:1186).

materiales tomados de la realidad, se había desvanecido, es cierto, con la
reaparición de la persona que fue como génesis de aquella creación de la
mente; pero el tipo, en su esencial e intachable belleza, subsistía vivo en
el pensamiento de la joven inválida. (3:417)

(It's true that the beautiful and perfect being that she loved, constructing
him herself with materials taken from reality, had vanished with the
reappearance of the person who was the source of that mental creation;
but the model, in its essential and exemplary beauty, subsisted in the
mind of the invalid young woman.)

This "tipo" comes to represent a transcendental ideal, a divinity that
the protagonist transforms into the object of worship.

As Tristana's amorous relationship with Horacio draws to a close, the
narrator refers to their past as "aquella novela" (that novel; 3:415). This
novel, which the narrator characterizes as "inverosímil y falsa" (unlifelike and false), describes the literary existence that the lovers have
invented for themselves. These words also call attention to the fictional
status of the text that we have been reading. Tristana is able to transcend the world that she has constructed only when she fully acknowledges the fictionality of this world by dispelling the notion of referentiality. Like Máximo Manso, who in the final chapter of *El amigo Manso*
looks down on the other characters of the novel as childish toys, the
narrator compares Tristana's fictions to "libros de entretenimiento que
nos han entusiasmado y enloquecido en la juventud" (books of entertainment that have enraptured and enchanted us in our youth; 3:415).
Tristana's self-consciousness—her distance from her fictions—also allows the reader of the novel to step back from the text and to view it as a
semiotic process.

After Horacio's final disappearance, Tristana increasingly removes
herself from all worldly concerns. Her isolation from the world becomes
so complete that she scarcely takes notice when her former lover abandons her (3:416). It is significant that she escapes into music, a non-
representational form of art. Pure art, represented by her new organ
(the musical instrument), replaces the old organ (the leg) that has tied
her to the referential world. Observing the religious fervor that trans-
ports Tristana to the realm of "idealidad dulcísima" (sweet ideality;
3:415), her organ teacher compares the protagonist to a saint. Tristana's
withdrawal from the world corresponds to the complete absence of her

voice from the text. The ironic narrator, who now dominates the narration, places himself at an increasing distance from the character. Rather than speaking from within her mind as he has often done before, he presents her primarily from an exterior perspective. At times, he even ironically adopts the views of her oppressor, Don Lope, or of society in general.

The narrator stands equally distant from Tristana's ideals and from society's norms, a detachment that contributes to the ambiguous implications of the novel's denouement. In the final chapter, Tristana submits, in silence, to marriage with Don Lope. Some critics have interpreted this outcome as a victory for the external world (whether this world is defined as "nature," society, or simply reality), which imposes its inexorable laws upon the individual who seeks an escape from these laws.[28] Germán Gullón, who approaches the novel from a metafictional perspective, sees Tristana's fate as a renunciation of the individual's fictions and a return to reality: "los personajes con resignación muestran su conformidad con el destino, y parecen entender que 'los sueños sueños son'" (the characters, with resignation, show their conformity to fate, and they seem to understand that "dreams are but dreams").[29] Another reader goes as far as to suggest that the protagonist has married willingly and that "she might even ('perhaps') be happy."[30] All of these critics seem to be convinced that the protagonist, willingly or otherwise, ultimately abandons her fictions and reconciles herself with the real world. Yet Tristana's absolute indifference to her situation suggests that she lives no longer in the world of reality: "Lo aceptó con indiferencia; había llegado a mirar todo lo terrestre con sumo desdén... Casi no se dio cuenta de que la casaron" (She accepted it with indifference; she had come to look at all earthly things with complete disdain... She almost didn't notice that they married her off; 3:418).[31] She has triumphed over reality by completely rejecting any link to it, an act that represents a logical culmination of her trajectory in the novel as creator of signs.

28. Feal Deibe, "*Tristana* de Galdós"; Livingstone, "The Law of Nature"; Miró, "*Tristana*."

29. "*Tristana*," 27.

30. Nimetz, *Humor in Galdós*, 90.

31. John Sinnigen, who interprets the novel from a strictly sociological perspective, also affirms that Tristana's "marriage cannot be seen as a reconciliation with society, for she continues to reject the social norm through her quest for an abstract ideal" ("Resistance and Rebellion in *Tristana*," 287).

In the final paragraph of *Tristana*, the narrator, who during previous moments has adopted the protagonist's perspective and has criticized Lope openly, now ironically identifies with the latter, who takes pleasure in his new life as Tristana's husband. The narrator's inconsistent vision makes it difficult for the reader to arrive at a clear-cut conclusion about the character's (or the implied author's) "feminism" or "antifeminism," as so many critics have tried to do. The ambiguity of the work culminates in the narrator's final words, "¿Eran felices uno y otro?... Tal vez" (Were they both happy?... Perhaps; 3:419), which express not so much his doubt as his wish to end the novel playfully on a note of indeterminacy. For the reader to speculate upon whether the characters do or do not "live happily ever after" would be as absurd as to believe that these characters have existed in real life. The significance of the ending lies not in the actual fate of the characters, but in the very fact of the novel's irresolution. The uncertainty of the conclusion, which reveals the narrator's unwillingness to tie up the loose ends of the text, subverts any attempt to find an unambiguous message in the novel.[32] Finally, the narrator's parody of the traditional fairy-tale ending (the protagonist marries the ogre rather than the prince) focuses the reader's attention on the literary nature of Tristana's story.

As she attempts to resolve the conflict between her belief in the power of language to beget reality and her denial of referentiality, Tristana defines the fictional process of the novel itself. Her efforts to gain autonomy as a woman by linguistically transforming her identity culminate in her rejection of society and of its language. Her final renunciation of the world corresponds to her literal exit from the novel, similar to the case of Maximiliano Rubín at the conclusion of *Fortunata y Jacinta*. It is paradoxical, then, that the dissolution of Tristana's feminist identity in *her* text marks her final birth as a self-sufficient and convincing character in *Galdós's* text. Tristana, the object of her self-creation, will always remain fully present in the reader's mind in the same way that Don Quixote, the knight-errant, continues to live for us even after he renounces his fictional identity on his deathbed.

In *Tristana*, as in the other two novels that we have examined, the character's struggle with the sign calls attention to the nature of the text

32. Diane Urey similarly examines the relationship between the "narrator of irony" and the ambiguous ending (frequent in Galdós's works), which "contributes to the over-all uncertainty of the reading process" (*Galdós and the Irony of Language*, 94).

as a sign that constantly reflects upon itself. In *La incógnita*, the subject of the following chapter, the protagonist's own writing mediates his reflection on the sign. His interpretive activity as a character in the text becomes inseparable from his act of narrative creation as the author of his epistles. Unlike Tristana's epistles, which occupy only a part of the work in which she appears, the letters of the narrator-protagonist of *La incógnita* actually become the novel that we are reading.

4

La incógnita and the Enigma of Writing

Manolo Infante's Interpretive Struggle

The writer can show only the *sign* without the *signified*: the world is a place endlessly open to signification but endlessly dissatisfied by it.

—Roland Barthes

In the final chapters of Galdós's epistolary novel *La incógnita*, the manuscript of Manolo Infante's letters is magically metamorphosed into its sequel, the dialogue-novel *Realidad*. Upon discovering this transfiguration, the author of the letters seeks in the second novel a possible solution to the interpretive impasse that he has reached in his quest for truth in *La incógnita*. In his final letter to Equis, the addressee of his correspondence and presumed author of *Realidad* within the text, Infante attempts to explain the significance of the newly transformed novel:

Tú, Equisillo diabólico, has sacado esta *Realidad* de los elementos indiciarios que yo te di, y ahora completas con la descripción interior del asunto la que yo te hice de la superficie del mismo. De modo que mis cartas no eran más que la mitad, o si quieres, el cuerpo, destinado a ser continente, pero aún vacío, de un ser para cuya creación me faltaban fuerzas. Mas vienes tú con la otra mitad, o sea con el alma; a la verdad aparente que a secas te referí, añades la verdad profunda, extraída del seno de las conciencias, y ya tenemos el ser completo y vivo. ¿Es esto así? (2:1218)

(You, diabolical Equisillo, have taken this *Realidad* from the circumstantial evidence I gave you, and now you complete with an interior description of this affair the surface one I furnished. So that my letters were no more than a part or, rather, the body, still empty, but destined to contain another being for whose creation I lacked strength. But you come with the other half, that is, with the soul; to the apparent truth that I reported to you plainly, you add the profound truth, extracted from the bosom of consciousness, and now we have a complete and living being. Isn't that so?)

Faced with this question, the reader of *La incógnita*, along with the narrator, is forced to ponder the relationship between the two novels. A number of critics have not hesitated to answer Infante's question affirmatively:[1] all agree that *Realidad* somehow completes an imperfect vision of reality that the first novel presents through the limited perspective of a single character. Others, however, have challenged such a reading of the two works, which not only privileges the second one but also denies *La incógnita* its independence from *Realidad*. Robert Russell, for example, observes that the second novel has no more claim to absolute truth than the first, since each of the texts presents perspectives that are lacking in the other: the essence of reality lies instead in the play of multiple perspectives.[2] Monroe Hafter likewise asserts that ironic reprise in *La incógnita* and *Realidad* subverts the reader's expectation of "disclosures or explanations" by leading him or her to an even more ambiguous reality.[3] Finally, Diane Urey interprets Manolo Infante's incapacity to attain knowledge of reality as a function of the ironic nature of all language: words, which "fold back upon themselves in a continuous play of unlimited significations," can have no reality beyond themselves.[4]

Each of these assessments reveals the choice that the reader has made between two antithetical ways of looking at language. The reading sustained by the first group of critics presupposes the referential function of language: *Realidad* represents the true referent behind the written text of *La incógnita*. The second interpretation, on the other hand, implies that language is autonomous, that there is no meaning behind

1. Laureano Bonet, *De Galdós a Robbe-Grillet*; Joaquín Casalduero, *Vida y obra de Galdós*; Gustavo Correa, *Realidad, ficción y símbolo en las novelas de Pérez Galdós*; Gonzalo Sobejano, "Forma literaria y sensibilidad social en *La incógnita* y *Realidad*, de Galdós."

2. "La óptica del novelista en *La incógnita* y *Realidad*."

3. "Ironic Reprise in Galdós' Novels," 237. Hafter refers to Livingstone's study as the theoretical basis for his discussion. According to Livingstone, the literary technique of "interior duplication"—a mirroring effect that blurs the separation between reality and illusion, life and art—is a manifestation of the "relativistic metaphysic" in the modern Spanish novel ("Interior Duplication and the Problem of Form in the Modern Spanish Novel").

4. *Galdós and the Irony of Language*, 94.

the written word. For these critics, *Realidad* is a further deferral of the truth that the first novel is unable to produce. The words *la incógnita* (enigma) and *realidad* (reality), which suggest, respectively, the absence and the presence of meaning, represent these two possible attitudes toward language: the reader may either privilege the second work based on the sequence of these titles or find irony in the apparent progression from uncertainty to truth.

La incógnita is highly self-conscious of its literary processes, of its nature as language: it dramatizes the tension between mimesis and autonomy, referentiality and self-referentiality.[5] Like many of the other Galdosian characters that we have seen, the protagonist of *La incógnita* is both an interpreter and creator of signs. Infante's meditation on language, however, is more explicit, for it takes the form of his own writing. In his letters, he inscribes the process of reconciling two contradictory visions of language. His search for a referent behind the sign (that is, his search for a solution to the various enigmas in the novel) inevitably comes into conflict with his role as inventor of the autonomous language of fiction. These opposing attitudes toward the sign, which form the basic semiotic paradigm in all of the works examined, also correspond to the two principal ways in which the critics have interpreted the relationship between *La incógnita* and *Realidad*.

The narrator of *La incógnita*, who comes to Madrid as a provincial *diputado*, transmits his observations of the society of Madrid to his friend Equis, who remains in the town of Orbajosa. Infante's words in his first letter reveal his sense of alienation from the language and conventions of the city:

Cierta aspereza que hay en mí, el desconocimiento de los convencionalismos de forma y de lenguaje imperantes en cada sociedad, el no saber encontrar la justa medida que aquí existe entre la etiqueta y la confianza, me han hecho aparecer un tanto desairado y cohibido en el salón de mi prima. (2:1121)

(A certain roughness about me, an ignorance of the conventions of form

---

5. Ricardo Gullón has written: "Esta novela no es una reflexión sobre sí misma; ni la época ni el autor favorecían tal designio" (This novel is not a reflection on itself; neither the epoch nor the author favored such an intention) (Introducción to *La incógnita*, 33). In his analysis of the novel's structure, however, he presents much evidence to the contrary.

and of language prevailing in each society, and an inability to find the exact proportion that exists here between formality and familiarity, have made me appear somewhat ungraceful and inhibited in my cousin's drawing room.)

His marginalization from the bourgeois society of Madrid (represented by his uncle's family and social connections) leads him constantly to scrutinize this society, both inside and outside his godfather's immediate household. As an interpretive frenzy overtakes Infante, every word or action of the people around him becomes an enigma, "una clave cifrada" (a ciphered code; 2:1139), that he must decipher. For the narrator of the novel, the act of writing represents the possibility of uncovering a true referent behind these enigmatic signs.

Although a desire for truth initially motivates Infante's interpretive activity, the instability of his vision of reality makes the knowledge of truth impossible. The letter form allows the reader to observe the evolution of the narrator's opinions as they change from day to day. Since the reader can know no more than what Infante sets down in writing at the end of each day, he or she shares the confusions and expectations of the narrator. In one of his letters, Manolo confesses the changeability of his opinions with respect to both politics and love, his primary obsessions:

> Desde que estoy en Madrid, es tal la movilidad de mis ideas, que me produce alarma . . . hay días que me despierto con las ilusiones democráticas más risueñas y angelicales que imaginarte puedes, y al siguiente cátame con sentimientos tan autoritarios, que me dan ganas de mirar como una bendición el palo del absolutismo . . . Pues en el orden afectivo, aquella impresionabilidad que tantas censuras y chanzas me ha valido de ti, también se ha recrudecido en vez de corregirse. (2:1141)

> (Since I've been in Madrid, the changeableness of my ideas is such that it alarms me . . . there are days when I wake up with the most pleasant and angelical dreams of democracy that you can imagine, and the next day here I am with such authoritarian sentiments that I feel like looking at the club of absolutism as a blessing . . . Well, in the emotional realm, that impressionability, which has merited so much censure and jest from you, has also gotten worse rather than being amended.)

In the first half of the novel, the question of Augusta's honor constitutes the principal enigma for Infante, who scrutinizes his cousin for signs of the truth:

Observo, reparo y escudriño en torno a ella, sospechando que podré descubrir algo que me asombre, y aunque nada veo, nada absolutamente más que una conducta pura y una reputación intachable, la *escama* persiste en mí y suspendo mi juicio. (2:1124)

(I observe, heed, and scrutinize her, suspecting that I'll discover something that surprises me, and although I see nothing, absolutely nothing other than innocent behavior and an irreproachable reputation, *mistrust* persists in me and I suspend my judgment.)

Yet this truth is never unambiguous. Infante's letters reveal radical changes in his opinion of Augusta from day to day: she is either the archetype of moral perfection or an unscrupulous adulteress. In one of his letters, he insists that his cousin is an angel ("es la pureza misma . . . ¡*Es un ángel!*" [she's chastity itself . . . She's an angel!; 2:1160]); however, a revelation that he experiences during a dreamlike state only a few days later ("La idea era ésta: 'Augusta no es honrada; Augusta tiene un amante' " [This was the idea: "Augusta isn't decent; Augusta has a lover"; 2:1166]) is enough to reverse his previous opinion. His inconsistency not only characterizes his attitude toward the object of his desire but also reveals his general tendency to view reality in terms of extremes. Augusta's husband Orozco is another "enigma moral" (moral enigma; 2:1175), whom the narrator sees as either a saint ("todo rectitud, nobleza y veracidad" [all rectitude, nobleness and truthfulness; 2:1123]) or a "vulgar misántropo" (vulgar misanthrope; 2:1174). Likewise, his opinion of Leonor wavers from one moment to the next: now she is a noble woman who is ever faithful to the memory of her friend Viera; now she is an indecent creature capable of selling this friendship for material gain. Despite Infante's claim to the veracity of his epistolary account, the constant fluctuations in his perception of reality call into question the notion of a stable truth.[6]

Manolo Infante's unreliability as narrator is a function of the linguistic nature of his desire: his writing dramatizes a circular process by

6. As Diane Urey asserts: "Words create reality, or rather they supplant it by their superimposition upon a reality which can never be known, if it exists at all" (*Galdós and the Irony of Language*, 85). Similarly, in her study of the evolution of the Spanish epistolary novel, Hazel Gold argues that *La incógnita* exemplifies the "realist author's increasing concern with the problematics of social, philosophical and linguistic intelligibility," communicating "the collapse of reality as a knowable construct" ("From Sensibility to Intelligibility," 134, 141).

which language produces desire, which, in turn, spurs further linguistic fabrications. As Girard points out, desire is always mediated by the Other, in whose image the subject creates him or herself.[7] In many self-conscious works of literature, this mediator, who comes to represent a quasi-divine figure for the subject, is the hero or heroine of another fictional text. The narrator of *La incógnita*, who recognizes the literary roots of his idealization of Augusta, writes to Equis: "no caen bien, en hombres de nuestra edad descreída, el misticismo amoroso de un Petrarca ni la fiebre de un Werther" (neither the amorous mysticism of a Petrarch nor the fever of a Werther is befitting of men in our unbelieving age; 2:1132).[8] By modeling his desire upon these archetypes, he transforms his own existence in imitation of a literary convention. Language becomes the means of closing the gap between the fictional Other and the real world to which the desiring subject belongs. It is interesting to note that Werther, a prototype of the romantic hero, is also the narrator of an epistolary novel: Infante thus imitates his mediator in more than one way.

In an effort to reach his literary ideal, the narrator fictionalizes not only the desired object but also the mediators of his desire: Orozco takes on the qualities of a saint, Malibrán is a perfect dandy, and Viera becomes a Calderonian hero. These Others, in turn, choose for the narrator the objects of his desire: in spite of Infante's obsession for Augusta during a large portion of the novel, the death of Viera, his mediator, causes him to lose interest in her; later in the novel, his desire for Leonor intensifies with the appearance of her lover. The narrator has no clear sense of himself precisely because the self is fictionalized and reinvented in relation to another, who in turn is a product of the imagination. The mutability of his opinions reveals the autonomous impulse in his language: his identity and that of others, as well as his account of each day's events, are all mediated by language, which creates its own reality.

Infante begins his first letter with the well-known topos of sincerity. His promise of complete honesty in exchange for Equis's confidentiality ("A cambio de la solemne promesa de tu discreción, nada te ocultaré, ni aun aquello que recelamos confiar verbalmente al amigo más íntimo" [In exchange for the solemn promise of your discretion, I won't hide

7. *Deceit, Desire and the Novel*, 1–52.

8. Ricardo Gullón employs Girard's theory to examine the mediated nature of Federico Viera's desire for Augusta in *Realidad* (Introducción to *Realidad*, 16–17).

anything from you, not even those things that we fear to entrust verbally to our closest friend; 2:1119]) constitutes an affirmation of the transparency of language, through which the narrator will capture reality and life, "descritas sin galanura, pero con veracidad" (described without elegance, but with truthfulness; 2:1119). Yet at the same time, he fears the artistic failure of his writing, which is meant to entertain its reader:

> Lo peor es que no sabré contar la historia de mi vida en Madrid de un modo que te interese y cautive. Ni poseo el arte de vestir con galas pintorescas la desnudez de la realidad, ni mi conciencia y mi estéril ingenio, ambos en perfecto acuerdo, me han de permitir invenciones que te entretengan con graciosos embustes. (2:1120)

> (The worst thing is that I won't know how to tell the story of my life in Madrid in a way that will interest and captivate you. I don't possess the art of clothing the nakedness of reality with a picturesque dress, nor will my conscience and my sterile wit, in perfect harmony with each other, permit fictions that will entertain you with charming lies.)

This passage reveals Infante's ambivalent attitude toward language. On the one hand, he regards language as clothing that conceals a true signified, "la desnudez de la realidad"; this reality, he implies, becomes transparent once the clothing is stripped away. His belief in a "naked" truth, however, is made ironic not only by his stated desire to entertain his correspondent, adorning this reality with "galas pintorescas," but also by his stylized language, which calls attention to itself. The narrator's awareness of the creative possibilities of language implicitly undermines his belief in the transparency of the sign.

Infante reveals his understanding of the autonomy of language during other moments of his first letter to Equis. As he begins his description of the characters who will later acquire importance in his narration, he refers to his inkwell, the metaphorical source of his artistic creation: "[Cisneros] me ha presentado a todos sus amigos, que son muchos, y entre los cuales hay algunos que no se me quedarán en el tintero" (He [Cisneros] has introduced me to all of his friends, who are many, and among them there are some that will not be left in my inkwell; 2:1120). By choosing this idiomatic expression, he exposes his characters' constitution as language, as drops of ink brought to life by the writer's pen.[9] Later in the same letter, he attributes his political success to his talent as creator of signs.[10] Upon facing an accusation of electoral fraud, the *diputado* extricates himself from this scandal through his linguistic skill. He composes a letter that, according to him, "ha sido muy elogiada por su lacónica dignidad y por las insinuaciones maliciosas que, en justo desquite, supe encajar en ella. Te la mando para que te rías un poco" (has been highly praised for its laconic dignity and for the malicious insinuations which, in fitting revenge, I inserted into it. I'm sending it to you so that you can laugh a little; 2:1121). In its context the letter is clearly a manipulation of the truth, an invention that the narrator has fabricated. Furthermore, the fact that Infante considers this letter to be a source of entertainment suggests that he is aware of its artistic nature. A similar fictional consciousness underlies his correspondence with Equis, which constitutes the material of *La incógnita*. It is therefore significant that Infante concludes his first letter to his friend by ironically questioning the discourse of history: "¿Crees tú que hubo romanos? Quita allá, bobo... Invenciones de los sabios para darse pisto" (You think there were Romans? Get out of here, simpleton... Inventions of scholars to put on airs; 2:1121). His distrust of even the most accepted form of language reveals his skepticism about the transparency of the sign. The fact that language can be used to lie suggests its essential duplicity, the lack of a natural motivation between the sign and its referent. As Umberto Eco has written: "if something [the sign] cannot be used to tell a lie, conversely it cannot be used to tell the truth: it cannot in fact be used 'to tell' at all."[11] If language can signify, it is potentially arbitrary.

As Infante continues his correspondence with Equis, he becomes increasingly conscious of the creative impulse in his writing. In a reference to his godfather Cisneros, for example, he exclaims to his friend:

9. The image of the inkwell recalls the scene of Máximo Manso's artistic birth in the first chapter of *El amigo Manso*. The author figure, who seeks Manso's collaboration in the creation of the novel, conjures the narrator-protagonist from a drop of ink: "Creo que me zambulló en una gota de tinta; que dio fuego a un papel; que después fuego, tinta y yo fuimos metidos y bien meneados en una redomita . . . Poco después salí de una llamarada roja, convertido en carne mortal" (I think that he plunged me into a drop of ink; set fire to a sheet of paper; and then the fire, the ink, and I were put into a little bottle and stirred up well . . . A bit later, I emerged from a flash of red flame, transformed into mortal flesh; 1:1186).

10. If language brings Infante political success, it is significant that his political fiasco at the end of the novel coincides with his failure as interpreter of signs.

11. *A Theory of Semiotics*, 7.

No te puedo expresar bien mis impresiones acerca de esta figura emi-
nentemente nacional. Trae a tu imaginación aquellos guerreros afeita-
dos que parecían curas . . . piensa en el obispo Acuña . . . reconstruye
el cuño de la raza y tipo de la madre Castilla, y podrás decir: "Vamos, ya
le tengo." (2:1122)

(I can't express to you very well my impressions of this eminently national figure. Call to your imagination those shaven warriors who looked
like priests . . . think of Bishop Acuña . . . reconstruct the mold and
lineage of mother Castile, and you can say: "There, now I have him.")

Recognizing that language is insufficient to express the reality that he
wishes to capture, Infante seeks Equis's collaboration in the creation of
his godfather. The narrator thus shows that language, rather than representing reality, begets it. In the next letter, he addresses his pen, which
has taken a life of its own: "Punto, punto aquí, ¡vive Dios! Pon un
punto como una casa, indiscreta pluma, o te estrello contra el papel" (A
period, a period here, for God's sake. Put down a period like a house,
indiscreet pen, or I'll smash you against the paper; 2:1125). His apos-
trophe, reminiscent of Cide Hamete's words to his pen at the end of *Don
Quixote*, dramatizes his loss of control over his own fictions. The independence of the writer's pen symbolizes the autonomy of the words that
it has traced on the page.

Infante's correspondent Equis collaborates actively in the act of narrative creation. As Janet Altman has shown, the explicit presence of the
narratee—that is, the recipient within the narrative—constitutes one of
the distinguishing characteristics of the epistolary form.[12] The epistolary novel partakes almost exclusively of the system of "discourse":[13]
the narrator (the "I") is constantly aware of the reader (the "you") that
he or she is addressing. Some have suggested that this reader, Equis, in
La incógnita is Manolo's second self or, at the least, another writer figure
within the text.[14] (Infante, in his first letter, refers to his correspondent's

12. *Epistolarity: Approaches to a Form*, 88. Prince defines the narratee in the following way: "All narration, whether it is oral or written, whether it recounts real or
mythical events, whether it tells a story or relates a simple sequence of actions in
time, presupposes not only (at least) one narrator but also (at least) one narratee, the
narratee being someone whom the narrator addresses" ("Introduction to the Study
of the Narratee," 7).

13. I adopt Emile Benveniste's term (*Problems in General Linguistics*, 208–9).

14. Gullón, Introducción to *La incógnita*, 16; Roberto Sánchez, *El teatro en la novela: Galdós y Clarín*, 133; Sobejano, "Forma literaria," 92–93.

fame as the author of certain "obras" [works; 2:1121].) Throughout the
novel, Infante shapes his narrative with the narratee's reaction in mind:
many times, he stops to address Equis's actual responses; at others, he
explains and justifies himself or even protests against the narratee's
potential objections. Although the reader does not directly see any of
Equis's letters until the end of the novel, the narratee, largely a product
of Infante's creation, emerges as a character in his own right. Manolo
portrays him as a mocking figure who assumes an attitude of superiority
and condescension toward him: direct addresses to the narratee, such as
"¿He dicho algún disparate?" (Have I made some foolish remark?;
2:1125) and "¿Qué te parece? ¿te ríes?" (What do you think? Are you
laughing?; 2:1135), abound in the letters. Equis is, above all, a dis-
believer who constantly questions the reliability of the epistolary account. The narrator, in turn, seeks to overcome Equis's disbelief through
his narrative art. His letters thus become an artistic game through
which he attempts to bring about the willing suspension of disbelief of
his correspondent and, by extension, of the reader of the novel. For
instance, after he sketches a linguistic portrait of Cisneros, he exclaims
to Equis, "No lo creas si no quieres, hombre sin fe" (Don't believe it if
you don't want to, man without faith; 2:1122), only to solicit, in the next
breath, the narratee's imaginative complicity in the creation of this
character. At other times, he casts Equis into the role of the "tonto"
(fool), who has been misled by an overactive imagination. Referring to
his rendezvous with La Peri, he declares to Equis:

> Creerás tú que el almuerzo acabó bien; que mi fascinación llegó a su
> apogeo, y que con el estímulo de los manjares y bebidas, me lancé a
> manifestar mis sentimientos, y alcé los amantes brazos y cayó en ellos *la
> Peri*, pagándome mi respetuosa afición con otra de la misma calidad o
> quizá menos pura? ¡Quiá, no seas tonto! Si te has creído esto, bórralo de
> tus papeles. (2:1192)

> (You must be thinking that lunch ended well; that my fascination reached
> its height and that with the stimulus of food and drinks I began to declare
> my feelings, and I raised my loving arms and Peri fell into them, return-
> ing my respectable fondness with another of the same class or perhaps
> less pure? Come now, don't be a fool! If you've believed this, erase it
> from your papers.)

(The reference to Equis's "papeles" evokes the image of a second writer who actively participates in the creative act.) Throughout this letter (Chapter 31), the narrator employs a similar strategy: he anticipates Equis's response only to discredit it. By creating a narrative that contradicts the narratee's expectations, he asserts his freedom as a writer. At the end of this letter, he offers an outline of the day's events as they might appear in headings of a serial novel published in a newspaper or a magazine: "Autopsia.—Entierro.—Mi pasión por *la Peri.*—Almuerzo en casa de ésta.—Amador.—La opinión pública o la confusión de las opiniones" (Autopsy.—Funeral.—My passion for Peri.—Lunch at her house.—Amador.—Public opinion or the confusion of opinions; 2:1194). This summary signals the narrator's awareness of the literary nature of his existence.

As the novel progresses, Infante's letters increasingly take on the quality of installments in a *folletín*. Consciously adopting the role of the serial story writer, he employs the techniques of suspension and continuation in order to maintain his reader's interest. In one letter, after having confessed his growing obsession with Augusta, he begins a commentary with the words, "De todo lo cual deduzco que..." (From all this I deduce that... ; 2:1133); but he leaves the statement in suspension and tauntingly exclaims to Equis:

Vete al diablo, que no tengo ganas de hacer deducciones ni de continuar esta deslavazada epístola. Estoy fatigado y de malísimo humor. ¿Te sabe a poco ésta? ¿Te deja a media miel? Pues fastídiate, y aguántate, y revienta. (2:1133)

(Go to the devil, since I don't feel like making deductions or continuing this impudent epistle. I'm exhausted and in a really bad mood. Does it seem insignificant to you? Does it leave you only half satisfied? Well, get irritated, bear it, and burst.)

On another occasion, he concludes a letter with the words "La contestación, *en el próximo núntero*" (The answer, *in the next issue*; 2:1168). The narratee, for his part, not only triggers Infante's correspondence in the first place, but also helps to move the narrative forward by his presumed curiosity. "Contén tu insana curiosidad" (Restrain your insane curiosity; 2:1124), "Ten un poco de paciencia" (Have a bit of patience; 2:1186), the narrator exclaims to his correspondent over and over again. The reader can never be sure whether Equis's impatience is actual or invented or whether, for that matter, he has any existence apart from Infante's imagination.

The narrator's ambivalent attitude toward the narratee reflects the basic ambiguity in his epistolary project: although he (presumably) invents Equis to make his letters seem real, this invented being exposes the ironic nature of his search for truth by calling attention to the literary nature of the letters. On one occasion, Manolo ridicules Equis's suggestion that he publish his letters as a *folletín*:

> ¿Qué tal? ¿Te resulta esto divertido, o te parece extravagante, empalagoso, digno sólo de figurar en el folletín de *El Impulsor Orbajosense*? Vamos, me ha hecho reír tu idea de que podría publicarse, trocando los nombres por otros extranjeros, suponiendo la acción en Varsovia y anunciando a la cabeza que es traducción del francés... Cállate la boca, o te estrello. (2:1168)

> (How is it? Does it seem entertaining to you, or extravagant and tiresome, worthy of appearing only in a serial story of *El Impulsor Orbajosense*? Come on, your idea has made me laugh, the idea that it could be published, exchanging the names for other foreign ones, imagining the action to be in Warsaw, and announcing in advance that it's a translation from French... Shut your mouth, or I'll smash you.)[15]

Infante expects the serial novel to produce a world that is remote and exotic: familiar names must be changed to foreign ones; the actions of the novel, to be entertaining, must take place on unfamiliar ground. His own account, he declares, captures an objective truth that remains untouched by "invención, intriga y todos los demás perendengues que las obras de entretenimiento requieren" (invention, intrigue, and all other trinkets that works of entertainment require; 2:1168). In a later letter, however, he expresses a desire to entertain his reader through the use of narrative artifice that he has previously rejected:

> se me ha pegado algo del amaneramiento artístico, y aspiro a excitar en

15. Infante's threat to smash his correspondent recalls his address to his pen earlier in the novel. It is as if Equis had begun to take control of the narration by reinventing it through his own language.

ti el interés de lector, contándote los hechos sin seguir la serie de los mismos, esto es, empezando por el medio, para caer luego en el principio y saltar de éste al final, concluyendo tal vez con vaguedades, interrogaciones o puntos suspensivos en que haya conjeturas para todos los gustos. (2:1194)

(some of the artistic affectation has rubbed off on me, and I aspire to arouse in you the interest of a reader, narrating events without following their order, that is, starting with the middle, then going on to the beginning, and jumping from there to the ending, concluding perhaps with vague remarks, interrogations, or suspension points in which there are conjectures for all tastes.)

By rejecting conventional narrative order, Infante undercuts his own claim to the objective representation of truth: mimesis becomes subservient to invention. His desire simultaneously to represent the truth and to exercise his artistic freedom reveals a contradictory vision of language. His search for truth through the act of writing presupposes a belief in the referentiality of language; at the same time, a belief in the autonomy of language underlies the artistic transformation of his letters into serial novel form.[16]

Infante attempts to escape this contradiction by blurring the line between life and literature. He explicitly compares the crime of *la calle del Baño* to the subject matter of a *folletín*: "Calderón es quien le lleva todas las noches las noticias más frescas, siempre estrambóticas, y al parecer tomadas de un folletín de Ponson du Terrail" (Calderón is the one who brings her, every night, the latest news, always bizarre, and apparently taken from a serial story by Ponson du Terrail; 2:1172). Just like the readers who anticipate the next installment of a serial novel, the

16. In her study of intertextuality in *Tormento*, Alicia Andreu views the Galdosian text as a play between two linguistic codes—"el folletinista y el realista" (that of the serial story and that of realism)—which deconstruct each other through mutual parody ("El folletín como intertexto en *Tormento*," 55). The novel, she claims, parodies the "imagination" of the *folletín*, which, in turn, undermines the "realist" text and its pretensions to truth. See also her *Galdós y la literatura popular*, a study with a more ideological focus in which she compares the moral ideology of two early *Novelas contemporáneas* to that of popular literature published in Madrid between 1840 and 1880. She shows that Galdós, through a critique of the bourgeois ideal of the "Mujer Virtuosa" (Virtuous Woman; 134), questions to a varying degree in these two novels the traditionalist ideology implicit in the popular literature of his times.

people of Madrid eagerly await new word on the murder. Life itself
becomes a text that each member of society sets out to decode by transforming himself or herself into a detective, and in the act of deciphering
the mystery each invents his or her own version of events. Infante sees in
these people a reflection of himself, who must struggle with his own
puzzle:

Mientras los demás roen el crimen, yo mastico mi enigma; digo, mío no,
de ella, y trato de dilucidar el arduo punto de quién será su cómplice. Mi
sumaria está tan embrollada como la del hecho de la calle del Baño, y a
cada hora veo una pista nueva. La sigo, y nada. (2:1172)

(While the others gnaw the crime, I ruminate my enigma; I mean, not
mine, but hers, and I try to clear up the difficult question of who might
be her accomplice. My proceedings are as confused as those of the event
in the calle del Baño, and each hour I see a new clue. I pursue it, and
nothing.)

Infante seeks to transform the absence of meaning (represented by *nada*)
into a presence—the truth—through the act of the imagination; likewise, the amateur sleuths in the crime of *la calle del Baño* fabricate their
own narratives in an attempt to solve the mystery. For both Infante and
the people around him, interpretation becomes an act of creation.

The frontier between life and literature becomes ever more hazy with
the discovery of Federico Viera's mysterious death in Chapter 28, a
"duplication" of the crime of *la calle del Baño*.[17] A violent and mysterious
death, associated with the world of the serial novel, becomes a part of

17. According to Ricardo Gullón, this "interior duplication" produces the effect
of "saturar el espacio novelesco de problematicidad y hacer sentir que la vida misma
es una incógnita, la última decisiva incógnita" (saturating the novelistic space with
problematicity and making it seem that life itself is an enigma, the ultimate decisive
enigma) (Introducción to *La incógnita*, 22). See Denah Lida for an account of Galdós's interest in "el crimen de la calle de Fuencarral" (the crime of Fuencarral
Street), on which he wrote articles for *La Prensa* of Buenos Aires (1888–1889). Lida
points out the parallels between Galdós's own chronicle of the crime and Infante's
references to "el crimen de la calle del Baño" (the crime of Baño Street)—and, later,
to the mysterious circumstances surrounding Viera's death—in *La incógnita* ("Galdós, entre crónica y novela").

everyday reality for Infante and for those around him.[18] The same
public that has participated in the "solving" of the first crime similarly
undertakes to decipher the enigma of Viera's death:

> Fácilmente comprenderás que un asunto de tal naturaleza, formado de
> misterio y escándalo, ha de excitar vivamente la chismografía de la raza
> más chismográfica del mundo; raza dotada de fecundidad prodigiosa
> para poner variantes a los hechos y adornarlos hasta que no los conoce la
> madre que los parió; raza esencialmente artista y plasmadora, que crea
> casos y caracteres, formando una realidad verosímil dentro y encima de
> la realidad auténtica. (2:1193–94)

> (You will easily understand that a matter of this nature, formed of mys-
> tery and scandal, is bound to excite keenly the gossip of the most gossipy
> people in the world; a people endowed with the prodigious fecundity to
> produce variations of events and to adorn them until even the mother
> who bore them will not recognize them; an essentially artistic and cre-
> ative people, which creates cases and characters, forming a lifelike real-
> ity within and above authentic reality.)

As society gives free rein to its artistic impulse, the narrator, in spite of
his imagination, redoubles his effort to uncover "la realidad auténtica."
However, he only becomes more deeply embroiled in his own confusion:
he is unable to attain this "realidad auténtica" because language mediates his knowledge of reality. As Cisneros declares to him, truth is
always a function of social and, therefore, arbitrary conventions: "La
santa verdad, hijo de mi alma, no la encontrarás nunca . . . Conténtate
con la verdad relativa y aparente, una verdad fundada en el honor . . .
El honor y las formas sociales nos imponen esa verdad, y a ella nos
atenemos" (You will never find, child of my soul, the sacred truth . . .
Be content with relative and apparent truth, a truth founded upon

18. Galdós's novel anticipates the detective fiction, a genre that is later to gain
popularity among the middle-class reading public. (See Todorov, who defines the
essence of the detective novel as its conformity to generic rules and conventions [*The
Poetics of Prose*, 42–52].) *La incógnita*, however, fails to provide the truth that is ex-
pected at the conclusion of a detective novel: the closure of the mystery is deferred to
Realidad, which in turn subverts the reader's expectations by revealing Viera's death
to be a suicide. The modern reader who consumes the two novels as a simple mystery
is sure to be disappointed by this anticlimactic solution.

honor . . . Honor and social forms impose that truth upon us, and we rely on it; 2:1197).[19] Just as the social code of honor impedes the discovery of "la santa verdad," the narrator's language—a product of literary conventions—forms a barrier between himself and the knowledge of truth.

Manolo's perception of reality is mediated not only by his fictions, but also by those of others around him, who weave their own texts in order to explain the mystery of Viera's death. Malibrán, who has mastered the language of social form and propriety, conforms to the role that Cisneros has assigned him and feigns ignorance of all knowledge that goes against the honor of his friend's family. Infante, who becomes increasingly frustrated in his desire to uncover the truth, sees Malibrán as a duplicitous sign: the language of social form—"las exterioridades más cultas" (the more refined exterior)—disguises his "falsedad y doblez" (falsity and duplicity; 2:1198).[20] For both Cisneros and Malibrán, social codes, deceptive as they may be, determine the nature of truth. La Peri, blackmailed and placed under pressure to explain the death of her lover, creates her "novelonas" (long novels; 2:1206) in order to deceive Infante and the authorities. Augusta stages a "drama" to conceal her true reaction to the event; Orozco, in turn, plays the role of a saint blissfully ignorant of his wife's possible involvement in his friend's death. Infante regards their behavior as a "papel bien estudiado y aprendido para embaucar al mundo" (well-studied and learned role to deceive the world; 2:1209). These various fictions, together with "las

19. In her study of *El amigo Manso*, Nancy Newton considers "the relativity of reality" to be one of the novel's primary concerns (*"El amigo Manso,"* 123). Galdós's preoccupation with this theme in *La incógnita*, as well as in many of his other works, can be seen in semiotic terms: the relativity of reality is a function of the conventionality of language itself.

20. Later, in *Realidad*, Malibrán himself asserts the deceptive nature of all social reality: "Hay dos esferas o mundos en la sociedad: el visible y el invisible, y rara es la persona que no desempeña un papel distinto en cada uno de ellos. Todos tenemos nuestros dos mundos, todos labramos nuestra esfera oculta, donde desmentimos el carácter y las virtudes que nos informan en la vida oficial y descubierta" (There are two spheres or worlds in society: the visible and the invisible, and there is rarely a person who doesn't perform a different role in each one of them. We all have our two worlds, we all cultivate our hidden sphere, where we prove false the character and the virtues that shape us in our official and public life; 2:1273). The gap between the visible and the invisible, the apparent and the real, reveals the character's consciousness of the arbitrariness of the social sign.

gárrulas novelas" (garrulous novels; 2:1201) invented by public gossip, confound his effort to arrive at the truth.

Faced with the knowledge that he may never solve the mystery, Infante nevertheless continues to defend the veracity of his epistolary account. In response to Equis's accusation that he has invented the figure of Cisneros, he declares: "No es Cisneros invención mía, ni yo invento nada. ¿Y qué iría ganando yo con meterme a plasmador, aunque hacerlo pudiera? Siempre me quedaría muy lejos de la realidad. ¡Esa sí que inventa, y con qué garbo!" (Cisneros is not my invention, nor do I invent anything. And what would I gain by becoming a creator, even if I could do it? I would always remain far from reality which, indeed, invents, and with what elegance!; 2:1197).[21] If his narrative appears to be fictional, he says, it is because life itself can resemble the world of literature: the writer's task is not to invent a fictional world, but to represent a reality that is already novelistic. Echoing Galdós's assertion in "Observaciones sobre la novela contemporánea en España" (Observations on the contemporary novel in Spain), he adds: "La invención realmente práctica consiste en abrir mucho los ojos y en acostumbrarse a ver bien lo que entre nosotros anda..." (Really practical invention consists in opening our eyes a lot and in getting accustomed to observe carefully what goes on around us... ; 2:1197).[22] Yet the very act of calling attention to Cisneros's inverisimilitude undermines his claim that he is simply recording his observations of the real world. Moreover, the literary nature of his conception of reality exposes the autonomy of

21. Infante's words are echoed in Augusta's reaction to the crime of *la calle del Baño* in *Realidad*: "Me inclino comúnmente a admitir lo extraordinario, porque de este modo me parece que interpreto mejor la realidad, que es la gran inventora, la artista siempre fecunda y original siempre" (I'm usually inclined to accept the extraordinary, because in this way it seems to me that I interpret reality better—reality, which is the great inventor, the always prolific and original artist; 2:1231). Life and literature become indistinguishable for Augusta, who interprets her world based on her reading of the *folletín*. Ironically, Infante, in the dialogue-novel, responds to Augusta by rejecting her "literary" interpretation of reality.

22. Infante here employs a similar argument by which Galdós, in his essay, defends "la novela de pura observación" (the novel of pure observation) against the "novela por entregas" (serial novel) (Pérez Galdós, *Ensayos de crítica literaria*, 118). Galdós's antithetical positioning of two kinds of novels and, hence, of two literary credos (the novel of observation—realism—versus the novel of the imagination—idealism) reveals his awareness of the tension between the referential and autonomous impulses of language.

the world that he presents within the text: what the narrator calls "reality" possesses fictional qualities because he, along with everyone else around him, perceives it in literary terms. As Oscar Wilde writes in "The Decay of Lying": "Life imitates art far more than art imitates life . . . Things are because we see them, and what we see, and how we see it, depends on the arts that have influenced us."[23] In other words, art— a fictional construct, a lie, to use Wilde's word—shapes our perception of reality. Just like the people who feel the effect of the London fog or the French sunlight in accordance with the impressionist painter's vision of these natural phenomena (examples given by Wilde's spokesperson), the narrator of *La incógnita* recreates his world through his knowledge of literature. Manolo Infante himself asserts: "El poeta precede al historiador, y anticipa al mundo las grandes verdades" (The poet precedes the historian, and anticipates great truths for the world; 2:1173), thus privileging the poet over the historian, creation over imitation.[24] The narrator adopts the role of the "poet" who transforms reality through language. During one of his final encounters with Augusta, he attempts to win her confidence by casting himself in the conventional role of the afflicted but faithful lover and by addressing her in the language of courtly love. After he completes his declaration of love, he exclaims to Equis: "¿Qué te parece la perorata, que no sé si he copiado con exactitud? Fastidiosa, ¿verdad?, y hasta un poquillo cursi" (How does this long speech seem to you, which I don't know if I've copied with exactness? Tedious, isn't it, and even a little tasteless?; 2:1210). He thus reveals an awareness of the conventionality of his words and actions. Yet soon afterwards, these empty words begin to produce genuine emotion in the narrator:

> Pues empecé a dirigirle aquellas frases amorosas que te he copiado, como quien emplea un argumento capcioso; se las dije, persuadido de que no decía la verdad, y al concluir, sorprendíme de ver que mi corazón respondía a todas aquellas retóricas con un sentimiento afirmativo. (2:1211)

23. "The Decay of Lying," 680–83.

24. Infante's words recall Aristotle's famous distinction between poetry and history: "poetry speaks more of universals, history of particulars" (*Poetics*, 33). By imitating not a fixed reality but a possible structure of events, the poet constructs new meanings through his or her art—he or she becomes the maker of the world.

(Well, I began to address to her those amorous phrases that I've copied for you, like a person who employs a captious argument; I said them to her, persuaded that I wasn't telling the truth, and upon finishing, I was surprised to see that my heart was responding to all that rhetoric with an affirmative feeling.)

Infante thus describes the process by which the empty sign becomes filled with meaning, as duplicitous language ("un argumento capcioso") eventually creates an authentic reality ("un sentimiento afirmativo").

The conflict between the narrator's original quest for truth and the autonomous impulse of his language inevitably leads to his interpretive crisis at the end of the novel. This crisis prompts Equis to participate in the deciphering of the unresolved enigmas by transforming Infante's letters (the text of *La incógnita*) into the dialogue-novel *Realidad*.[25] Ironically the narrator (who asserts his authorial power at the beginning of the novel by claiming to his correspondent: "Hemos cambiado nuestros papeles . . . Yo resucito, y tú mueres; yo salgo a la luz, y tú caes en ese pozo de ignorancia, malicia y salvaje ruindad" [We've changed our roles . . . I come back to life, and you die; I come out into the light, and you fall into that well of ignorance, malice and untamed baseness; 2:1119]) ultimately yields his author-ity to his epistolary rival. Equis's letter to Infante in the final chapter (significantly, the only letter of Equis that the reader sees directly) marks his birth as the second author of the novel. In this epistle, he reveals the process by which his friend's letters have metamorphosed into *Realidad*, presumably the completed version of *La incógnita*. Anticipating Infante's doubt, he declares:

El fenómeno que hoy admiras es tan natural como el más corriente que en la Naturaleza puedes advertir uno y otro día. Cuando quiero obtener la verdad de un caso, cojo los datos aparentes y públicos, los escribo en

25. This transformation from writing (*La incógnita*) to speech (*Realidad*) and the critics' tendency to privilege dialogue over the written form can be seen as a manifestation of what Derrida has called the "metaphysics of presence" (*Of Grammatology*, 22). According to Derrida, spoken language produces a false link between the logos and the origin of truth through the presence of the speaking subject, whereas writing is predicated on an absence of original meaning. If we interpret the response to Galdós's two works in these terms, it is paradoxical that *Realidad* is actually a written text, which leads us to a further deferral of the truth.

varias hojas de papel, los meto en el arca de los ajos, y a los tres días, hora más, hora menos, ya está hecho. (2:1218)

(The phenomenon that you're marveling at today is as natural as the most commonplace one that you observe in Nature from one day to the next. When I want to get at the truth of a matter, I take the apparent and public information, I write it down on various sheets of paper, I put them in the garlic chest, and in three days, more or less, it's all done.)

Equis suggests that *Realidad* has come into being through a natural process (represented by the image of the garlic) and that it is therefore truth itself. Yet the very idea of a magical transformation undercuts his claim that his text represents the inner truth that has remained hidden to Infante in *La incógnita*. The fact that Equis himself provides the two versions of the novel with their respective titles, thereby creating the opposition between "enigma" and "truth," suggests that he has reinvented Infante's narrative.

As the reader continues to the second novel, he or she discovers that the dialogue novel does not simply present the same events and characters of *La incógnita* from a different angle. Equis's novel, which revolves around the events immediately preceding and following Viera's death, covers a significantly shorter time span than Infante's account. The importance given to particular characters in the two novels is also different: Orozco and Viera come to the foreground in the sequel, whereas Infante disappears almost completely from the scene. Finally, the dialogue-novel presents new enigmas for the reader in search of a solution to the unanswered questions of *La incógnita*. Clarín, who reads *Realidad* principally as a psychological novel, blames the novel's alleged failure to capture the inner truth of the characters' psyche on the artificiality of Galdós's use of the dialogue form.[26] What Clarín sees as a formal deficiency, however, serves as a vehicle for the novel's perspectivist vision. The dialogue novel, rather than bringing the reader closer to a reality, psychological or otherwise, makes the truth more elusive by introducing a greater number of voices and perspectives.[27] For Roberto

26. Leopoldo Alas, *Galdós*, 201–2.

27. In his prologue to *El abuelo*, Galdós himself lays bare the illusory nature of the dialogue form, which makes the reader believe that what he or she sees is a direct imitation of reality: behind this "ingeniosa imitación de la Naturaleza" (ingenious imitation of Nature) is an "artista oculto" (hidden artist; 3:801), who shapes the reader's perception of this reality.

Sánchez, dialogue helps to reproduce the social fictions ("pequeñas comedias de disimulo y engaño" [small comedies of dissimulation and deception]) that the hypocritical characters act out in their daily lives; truth, therefore, remains concealed behind social masks and formulas.[28] The theatrical nature of the characters' everyday existence, reflected in the dialogue form, reveals the duplicitous nature of the social sign, which never corresponds to what it seems to signify.

The notion of truth becomes more ambiguous as each character in *Realidad* interprets and recreates the world according to his or her own fictions.[29] Augusta, like Flaubert's Emma Bovary, constantly seeks in life the extraordinary ("lances dramáticos" [dramatic episodes] and "misterios de folletín" [mysteries of the serial story; 2:1229]) that conforms to the world of popular literature. Through her knowledge of the *folletín*, she transforms the crime of *la calle del Baño* into a drama of love and intrigue, inventing a stepmother and various influential personages to figure in her fiction. On another occasion, she declares that Viera's sister's elopement with the store clerk is "hasta poética" (even poetic; 2:1269). Moreover, Augusta's vision of her lover is shaped by literary conventions, as Viera himself recognizes: "lo que ignoras de mí se revela a tu imaginación soñadora como algo interesante, novelesco, dramático" (what you don't know about me becomes revealed in your dreamy imagination as something interesting, novelistic, dramatic; 2:1257). Not only does Augusta idealize her lover, but she imagines her romance to conform to the formula of the *folletín*: it is significant that upon witnessing Viera's suicide, she grieves over the antiromantic conclusion of her illicit love affair rather than over her lover's actual death.

Federico Viera, in turn, lives his life according to an anachronistic concept of honor, which evokes Calderón's honor plays.[30] Clotilde's

---

28. *El teatro en la novela*, 139.

29. For Gerald Gillespie, the creative activity of these characters has existential implications. As they escape into their own fictions, they become increasingly alienated from one another and from the outside world. The instability of reality is therefore a function of the characters' psychological and existential evolution: "In their world truth is not fixed; it changes with their groping, and in a sense, they are producing it as they move along the pathways of the psyche, rather than 'discovering' it" ("Reality and Fiction in the Novels of Galdós," 26).

30. Viera's fiction is similar to that of the equally quixotic count of Albrit (*El abuelo*), whose search for his "true" granddaughter is also based on an antiquated code of honor: the belief that the condition of "limpieza del nombre y de la sangre" (purity of name and blood; 3:844) corresponds to the individual's moral worth.

engagement to a man of a lower social class sends him into despair, for the fallen aristocrat sees the action of his sister as a violation of this code. As those around him note, Viera's concept of honor is a product of social and literary conventions: "Este señorito fantasioso cree que estamos en tiempos como los de esas comedias en que salen las cómicas con manto, y los cómicos con aquellas espadas tan largas, y hablando en consonancia. ¡Válgate Dios con la quijotería!" (This vain master believes that we are in the times of those plays in which actresses with gowns and actors with those long swords appear, speaking in rhyme. God help you with this quixotism!; 2:1248). Viera soon becomes an enigma to himself, as he loses his capacity to distinguish his true self from the conventional roles that he has adopted. Even in his soliloquies, he poses further questions on the nature of reality rather than unveiling inner truths.[31] On one occasion he asks himself: "Hay en mí dos hombres, el Federico Viera que todo el mundo conoce, y el amigo de 'La Peri.' ¿Cuál es el verdadero y cuál el falsificado?" (There are two men in me, the Federico Viera that everyone knows, and the friend of "La Peri." Which one is the true and which one the false?; 2:1252). The tension between these two selves implies, once again, a conflict between two ways of perceiving the sign: the social self is an arbitrary sign and therefore appears to be false; the hidden self ("el amigo de La Peri"), which exists independently of social conventions, seems to represent a true self. Yet seen from within society's system of signs, the false is the true, and the true is the false. Viera's consciousness of the conventionality of language leads him to aspire to an ideal of pure fiction: it is, significantly, his own creation—Orozco's Shadow—that seduces him away from the "convencionalismos pueriles" (puerile conventionalisms; 2:1309) of society toward the "esfera de las ideas puras" (sphere of pure ideas; 2:1308). His encounter with the Shadow leads him to doubt again his own sense of reality:

Albrit, unlike Viera, remains unaware of the conventionality of this social code ("la suprema ley del honor" [the supreme law of honor; 3:820]) until the final moment of the novel: the count's illegitimate granddaughter turns out to be more morally worthy than the legitimate one. The outcome of Albrit's search, together with the concluding remark of the children's tutor, "El mal... ¿es el bien?" (Evil... is it good?) challenge the notion of an absolute truth attainable through language (3:904).

31. Sobejano, who claims, "El soliloquio no denota disimulo, sino que por el contrario es una forma de buscar directamente la propia verdad" (Soliloquy does not indicate dissimulation; on the contrary, it is a way of searching directly for truth itself), fails to note that this "truth" often contains further ambiguities ("Forma literaria," 101).

¿He hablado yo con Orozco en casa de San Salomón, o es ficción y supercheria de mi mente? . . . La realidad del hecho en mí la siento; pero este fenómeno interno ¿es lo que vulgarmente llamamos realidad? Lo que yo he dicho cien veces: no hay bastantes palabras para expresar las ideas, y deben inventarse muchas, pero muchas más. (2:1306)

(Have I spoken to Orozco in the house of San Salomón, or is it a fiction and trickery of my mind? . . . I feel the reality of facts in me; but is this internal phenomenon what we commonly call reality? What I've said a hundred times: there aren't enough words to express ideas, and more words should be invented, many more.)

To perceive the inadequacy of language—that is, the gap between the signifier and the signified—is to acknowledge its essential arbitrariness. The idea of a perfect language that can close this gap by expressing the inexpressible is in itself a fiction, a pretext for the character's inventive acts. In the context of his linguistic struggle, Viera's suicide represents the final triumph of his fictions, an affirmation of the autonomy of language.

Yet another key figure of *Realidad*, Tomás Orozco, lives his life according to an ideal system of thought that he has invented ("este sistema... , lo llamaré religioso... , en este sistema que me he formado, sin auxilio de nadie, sin abrir un libro, indagando en mi conciencia los fundamentos del bien y del mal" [this system... , I'll call it a religious one... , this system I've formed for myself without anyone's help, without opening a book, examining my conscience for the foundations of good and of evil; 2:1237]). Having transformed himself into an enigma undecipherable by society's conventions, he becomes the object of interpretation for those around him: Augusta, who regards him as a "jeroglífico" (hieroglyphic; 2:1327), asks herself whether her husband is a saint or a madman; Joaquín Viera looks for a scheming egoist behind Orozco's exterior mask; and society scrutinizes him during the days following Federico's death as if he were "un folletín espeluznante" (a terrifying serial story; 2:1323).[32] Throughout *Realidad* Orozco aspires to his ideal, and in the final scene of the novel, having freed his fiction from society, he stands face to face with the incarnation of his "idea," the Image of the late Viera. Orozco, who celebrates his communion with

32. Arnold Penuel, who takes a thematic approach to Orozco's enigma, sees in the ambiguity of the character's virtue a statement on "the complexity and elusiveness of reality" ("The Ambiguity of Orozco's Virtue," 412).

this Image in the autonomous world of fiction, recognizes that language, rather than uncovering the truth, must create it: "No puedo decir que poseo la verdad; pero tengo una idea, interpretación propiamente mía, hija de mi perspicacia y de mi estudio de la conciencia universal e individual" (I can't say that I possess the truth; but I have an idea, my own interpretation, child of my perspicacity and of my study of universal and individual conscience; 2:1333).

These characters constantly transform themselves and the world around them based on individual and/or social fictions. As these fictions take on lives of their own, reality and illusion, life and literature become increasingly indistinguishable. *Realidad* therefore leads not to a simple truth but to further mysteries and ambiguities on all levels of meaning—the social, psychological, existential, literary, and linguistic. Given this fact, the magical transformation of Infante's letters into the dialogue-novel symbolizes the autonomy of the language of fiction rather than its enslavement to truth.[33] Equis, through an act of the imagination, rewrites his friend's narrative: the novel that emerges from the chest is the joint creation of the two characters. Significantly, neither Infante nor Equis considers the handwriting of *Realidad* to be his own: for Infante, it is Equis's handwriting disfigured; Equis, in turn, claims that the writing is Infante's own. This confusion suggests that the dialogue-novel belongs not just to Equis, but to both writers, who are mutually dependent in their creative activity.

Equis, in his letter, reveals an awareness of the paradox of fiction by dramatizing the tension between deliberately self-conscious writing and writing that effaces its own condition as language. On the one hand, he creates the illusion of a reality that simply *is*, a reality that is unmediated by language: "La realidad no necesita que nadie la componga; se compone ella sola" (Reality doesn't need anyone to compose it; it composes itself; 2:1218). Yet in the next breath, he makes this assertion ironic by declaring to Infante: "Pues si quieres que yo te crea tu pasión por Augusta, tienes que creerme la sobrenatural y ajosa metamorfosis de tus cartas en novela dramática" (Well, if you want me to believe your passion for Augusta, you have to believe the supernatural and garlicky

---

33. Angel Tarrío's claim that *La incógnita*, together with *Realidad*, constitutes "un manifiesto realista" (a realist manifesto) is therefore misleading. According to Tarrío, Equis, an alter ego of Galdós, leads Infante to "la objetiva versión de la verdad narrada" (the objective version of the truth that was narrated) by transforming him into the reader of his own narrative (*Lectura semiológica de Fortunata y Jacinta*, 77).

metamorphosis of your letters into a dramatic novel; 2:1218–19).[34] Not only does Equis lay bare the fictionality of his creation by asking his correspondent to suspend his disbelief, but he also reveals the autonomy of Infante's writing by placing both fictions on the same plane. Fully aware of the paradox of language, Equis continues on another level Infante's struggle to reconcile the two opposing visions of the sign.

La incógnita exemplifies a subversion of what Roland Barthes calls the "hermeneutic narrative, in which truth predicates an incomplete subject, based on expectation and desire for its imminent closure."[35] Each successive letter of Infante, rather than moving the reader toward the solution of the original enigma, sets up further snares and complications. These knots, formed by the various narrative threads in the novel, are never untied. The impasse at the conclusion of the novel gives rise to yet another enigma, the meaning of *Realidad*. Equis defers the solution of the "incógnitas" to the magically produced dialogue-novel; yet the "answers" that the reader finds in the second novel are limited to the clarification of the events leading up to Viera's death. Many of Infante's other questions remain unanswered, partly because he has never clearly defined the "incógnitas" in the first place. The central enigma of *La incógnita*, composed of the sum of all the unknowns, concerns the nature of Infante's quest for truth. *Realidad*, in its failure to provide an answer, embarks the reader upon yet another interpretive journey. The solution to the enigma of writing is infinitely deferred, for the ultimate meaning of the quest is to be found in the quest itself.[36]

34. Equis's declaration is a clear echo of Don Quixote's words to Sancho Panza after the squire returns from his imaginary voyage on the Clavileño: "—Sancho, pues vos queréis que se os crea lo que habéis visto en el cielo, yo quiero que vos me creáis a mílo que vi en la cueva de Montesinos" (Sancho, since you want us to believe what you saw in the sky, I want you to believe what I saw in the cave of Montesinos; *Don Quijote*, 2:355). In both works, the fictional contract between two creators demands a mutual suspension of disbelief.

35. *S/Z*, 76.

36. Todorov interprets Henry James's short story, "The Figure in the Carpet" (1896), in precisely these terms (*The Poetics of Prose*, 177). James's tale dramatizes a young critic's quest for the true meaning of a renowned writer's literary work: this meaning turns out to be the quest itself—the perpetual search for the absent "figure in the carpet." The parallel in the literary preoccupations of these contemporaneous authors is worthy of note.

5

History as Language in the First Series of the *Episodios nacionales*

The Literary Self-Creation of Gabriel de Araceli

Las letras pasaban por mi mano, trocándose de brutal y muda materia en elocuente lenguaje escrito. ¡Cuánta animación en aquella masa caótica! En la caja, cada signo parecía representar los elementos de la creación, arrojados aquí y allí, antes de empezar la grande obra.

—*El 19 de marzo y el 2 de mayo*

(The letters passed through my hand, being converted from raw and silent material into eloquent written language. How much animation there was in that chaotic mass! In the box, each sign seemed to represent the elements of creation, strewn here and there, before the beginning of the great work.)

The study of four *Novelas españolas contemporáneas* in the preceding chapters reveals that those novels are highly conscious of their own status as fiction and as language. As the survey of critical sources indicates, an increasing number of *galdosistas* are taking on the task of exploring the self-conscious nature of these works. In contrast to the *Novelas españolas contemporáneas*, however, the *Episodios nacionales* have received little attention from modern critical perspectives.[1] With only a few exceptions, scholars have overlooked the literary and linguistic dimensions of Galdós's "historical novels," limiting criticism on these

1. A significant exception is Diane Urey's recent book, *The Novel Histories of Galdós*, which appeared after the original version of this manuscript was completed. This seminal study revindicates the literary value of the *Episodios* by proposing that Galdós's art, "whether labeled historical or contemporary novels," be studied as "a system of language" (9). By examining Galdós's late *Episodios* primarily as literary and linguistic artifacts, Urey not only rectifies the critical bias against these novels, traditionally considered to be lacking in literary value, but also redefines the categories of "history" and "novel" based on Galdós's practice of a highly experimental historical fiction. Urey currently has another volume in progress on the early historical novels of Galdós.

novels, especially on the first series, primarily to sociological investiga-
tions.[2] Hans Hinterhäuser, one of the first to author a book-length
study of the *Episodios*, attempts to piece together Galdós's vision of
history by referring to the author's biography and to the possible sources
for his works. Antonio Regalado García reduces all of Galdós's historical
novels to the author's political ideology. Yet another critic, influenced by
Lukács's model of the historical novel, views the *Episodios* as a document
of social and historical evolution.[3] Even Brian Dendle, who recognizes
the importance of the fictional elements in these novels, considers these
elements in a predominantly negative light, as an unintentional subversion of Galdós's historical vision.[4]

2. Nigel Glendinning's study of the psychological and moral motivation of characters in the first series exemplifies another thematic approach that disregards the
linguistic constitution of the text. He treats the protagonists of these works not as
fictional characters, but as "individual human beings" ("Psychology and Politics in
the First Series of the *Episodios nacionales*," 56).

3. Alfred Rodríguez, *An Introduction to the Episodios Nacionales of Galdós*. For
Lukács, the rise of the historical novel in the early nineteenth century marks the
emergence of a new historical consciousness among writers. The modern historical
novel focuses upon a complete society as the object of artistic representation, presents history as a process of continual evolution through which the past becomes the
precondition of the present, and portrays the individual as the product of his or her
age and of a concrete historical destiny (*The Historical Novel*). Lukács's conception of
the modern historical novel can be compared to Erich Auerbach's characterization of
modern realism as "the serious treatment of everyday reality, the rise of more extensive and socially inferior human groups to the position of subject matter for prob-
lematic-existential representation, on the one hand; on the other, the embedding of
random persons and events in the general course of contemporary history, the fluid
historical background" (*Mimesis: The Representation of Reality in Western Literature*,
491). Significantly, the idea of mimesis, or representation, forms the basis of both the
historical novel and the realist novel.

4. In his discussion of *Trafalgar*, for example, Dendle attributes what he views as
Galdós's incomplete vision of history to the literary aspects of the novel: "The clumsy
attempts at amusing the reader with the portrayal of the implausibly comic and with
the adoption of a narrative method that ostentatiously uses the devices of fictional
models impede suspension of disbelief." Later in his conclusion, he claims: "The
overloading of events and characters, the caricatures, the symbolic names, and the
quite obviously biased vision of history immediately indicate that we are reading
fiction, not historical recreation" (*Galdós: The Early Historical Novels*, 33, 163).
Dendle's criticism of Galdós's "unrealistic" rendering of history assumes the existence of an objective reality attainable through language. The *Episodios*, by dramatizing the inseparability of "history" and "fiction" in the text, question the notion of
accurate historical recreation.

Many of these critics have approached the *Episodios* with the intention
of uncovering historical truth or, at the least, a political ideology that
they believe these texts represent. Yet historical writing, as Hayden
White shows, is ultimately a linguistic structure that the historian constructs through the use of the poetic imagination: "a verbal structure in
the form of a narrative prose discourse that purports to be a model, or
icon, of past structures and processes in the interest of *explaining what they
were by representing them.*" The process of narrativization, or "emplot-
ment," as White would call it, naturally involves the imposition of an
artistic order on historical events. Yet at the same time, the presentation
of a set of events "as a comprehensible process with a beginning, middle, and end" implicitly lends authority to the historical discourse.[5]

Galdós's *Episodios nacionales* question the traditional notion of historical discourse as transparent language by calling attention to their identity as a conventional system of signs. The linguistic and literary nature
of these novels is made explicit by the presence of a fictional narrator
who mediates between the reader and the history within the text.[6] As
Ricardo Gullón observes, sociological critics, all too eager to reconstruct the author's vision of history, have repeatedly ignored the autonomy of the narrator, who invents his version of history.[7] Galdós's *Episodios*, commonly considered as "historical novels" in the Lukácsian
sense, often expose historical writing to be an act of creation.[8] These

5. *Metahistory: The Historical Imagination in Nineteenth-Century Europe*, 2 (emphasis
White's), 7. See also White's discussion of the relationship between narrative discourse and historical representation in his essay "The Value of Narrativity in the
Representation of Reality" (*The Content of the Form*, 1–25). According to White, the
narrative "form" that historical discourse takes possesses an implicit moral or ideological "content" in its own right rather than being a value-free medium for the
representation of history. Narrativity, as the precondition for the authority of the
historical discourse, actually helps to *create* historical meaning.

6. Diane Urey, in "Linguistic Mediation in the *Episodios Nacionales* of Galdós:
Vergara," similarly asserts that the meaning of a historical novel, like that of any other
work of fiction, "is only obtained mediately—through the medium of language—
whether it be the language of the text of the printed page, or that which the reader
himself brings to the text" (263). See also Urey's "The Confusion and the Fusion of
History and Fiction in the Third Series of Galdós' *Episodios Nacionales*."

7. "Los *Episodios*: la primera serie," 299.

8. Germán Gullón also recognizes that the writing of history is a literary under-
taking: "Galdós va a narrativizar la historia dándole forma novelesca, literaturizán-
dola, y en verdad poniéndola al servicio de la ficción" (Galdós will narrativize history, giving it novelistic form, "literaturizing" it, and truly putting it to the service of
fiction) ("Narrativizando la historia: *La corte de Carlos IV*," 46).

novels blur the separation between "history" and "fiction" through their awareness that history is ultimately language and that, as such, it can exist only as the written word of a narrator.[9]

The fictional narrator of the entire first series of the *Episodios* is the adult Gabriel de Araceli, whose writings are an account of his participation in the major events of Spanish history between the Battle of Trafalgar (1805) and the end of the Napoleonic invasion (1813). As is true with all autobiographical accounts, the narrative arises out of the space between the writing subject (the adult Araceli) and the written self (the protagonist of the events narrated).[10] In writing a personal and national history, Gabriel de Araceli repeatedly calls attention to his role as inventor of fictions, of which his written self forms a part. The entire notion of historical reconstruction is therefore undermined not only by the mediatory presence of a fictional narrator, but also by his awareness of the fictionality of his narrative.

Gabriel de Araceli's self-creation in the first series of the *Episodios* depends directly upon the transformation of his semiotic consciousness: the protagonist, who at first maintains a fundamentally innocent vision of the signs of the world around him, gradually learns to become an actor in this world by learning to manipulate its duplicitous signs. *La corte de Carlos IV*, the second novel of this series, marks the protagonist's awakening to the arbitrary nature of the sign through his contact with the courtly society of Madrid, represented by the metaphor of the theater. Although Gabriel's education in the world does not stop at the end of this novel, his increasingly sophisticated vision of the sign later in the first series is a result of his role as actor—in theater and society alike—in *La corte de Carlos IV*. His mastery of language enables him to create narratives through which he learns to deceive and to control others around him. Finally, his semiotic education, which begins in this second novel, is completed only through the act of writing his autobiogra-

9. Another instructive study by Diane Urey is "Isabel II and Historical Truth in the Fourth Series of Galdós' *Episodios Nacionales*," in which she examines these works as a self-conscious commentary on the process of the historical novel itself. By analyzing the role of Pepe Fajardo, the historian figure within the text, Urey demonstrates that these works ultimately undermine the historian's claim to truth behind the written word.

10. Harry Sieber, in his work on *Lazarillo de Tormes*, describes the twofold structure of the picaresque narrative in precisely these terms and highlights the importance of this structure for his interpretation of the novel as an account of the protagonist's semiotic initiation (*Language and Society in "La vida de Lazarillo de Tormes"*).

phy. It is possible, therefore, to read the novels of the entire first series as a self-conscious account of the protagonist-narrator's semiotic initiation, which culminates in the writing of his memoirs. By viewing these works from this perspective, one can justify Galdós's use of the first-person narrative, which Dendle criticizes as lacking in coherence and in plausibility.[11]

In the opening pages of *La corte de Carlos IV*, Gabriel, having abandoned his position in Cádiz as Don Alonso's page, enters the service of an actress, Pepa González, in Madrid. Not yet wise in the ways of the world, he is cast into the center of the intrigues and conspiracies of the "inhospitalaria Corte" (inhospitable Court; 1:255).[12] Pepa's profession is in itself significant, as acting involves the fabrication of signs that are meant to deceive the spectators, drawing them into the artistic illusion—an illusion that leads them to believe that the signs on stage correspond to a referent in the real world when such a referent does not really exist. Gabriel declares that his occupation, which brings him into close contact with this world of artifice, "era muy propio para adquirir conocimiento del mundo en poco tiempo" (was very suitable for gaining knowledge of the world in a short time; 1:255). Throughout the novel, the narrator associates theater with the falseness of courtly society, whose signs never correspond to the truth. The king, apparently the head of state, is a puppet of the opportunistic Godoy; the queen, whose hypocrisy is represented by her false teeth, "engaña al pueblo, haciendo creer lo que no es" (deceives the people, making them believe what is not true; 1:312), as one of her servants observes; the ministers, according to the Countess Amaranta, are no more than "instrumentos y maniquíes que se mueven a impulsos de una fuerza que el público no ve" (instruments and puppets that move to the promptings of a force that the public doesn't see; 1:316); even the Cortes of Cádiz are compared to a farce, "una función de teatro" (a theatrical performance; 1:901), by one of their spectators.[13]

11. *Galdós*, 32–33.

12. Benito Pérez Galdós, *Obras completas (Episodios nacionales)*. All subsequent references to the *Episodios* will appear in the text within parentheses.

13. Brian Dendle observes: "Falsehood exists not only in the theater; it pervades the national life of Spain . . . Ministers appear to rule, but they are puppets manipulated by the hidden intrigues of courtiers. The royal family heads the nation, but the queen herself is the victim of blackmail. As in a bad comedy, rewards and punishments are capriciously granted. While courtiers play their fickle roles, the real power—that of Napoleon, to whose tune all must ultimately dance—lurks offstage" (*Galdós*, 36).

Pepa González herself, as the adult narrator recalls her, is a duplicitous sign, which language is unable to represent:

> caigo también en que sus movimientos tenían una gracia especial, un
> cierto no sé qué, un encanto indefinible, que podrá expresarse cuando el
> lenguaje tenga la riqueza suficiente para poder designar con una misma
> palabra la malicia y el recato, la modestia y la provocación. (1:256)

> (I also realize that her movements had a special charm, a certain some-
> thing, an indefinable delight, which can be expressed only when lan-
> guage has sufficient richness to be able to designate with the same word
> malice and discretion, modesty and provocation.)

In his self-conscious meditation upon his language, the narrator recognizes the reversibility of these antithetical words. If language is insufficient in capturing the duplicitous nature of Pepa's character, he suggests, it is because all signs are reversible and, therefore, arbitrary:
"Esta rarísima antítesis consiste en que nada hay más hipócrita que
ciertas formas de compostura, o en que la malignidad ha descubierto
que el mejor medio de vencer a la modestia es imitarla" (This very rare
antithesis consists in the fact that there's nothing more hypocritical than
certain forms of circumspection, or that malignity has revealed that the
best way to conquer modesty is to imitate it; 1:256). His recognition of
the insufficiency of language allows him to manipulate social signs
through an act of imitation and gradually to replace these signs with an
autonomous language of his own making.

The reader perceives a constant tension between the adult writer's
awareness of the arbitrary nature of language and the innocence of the
adolescent protagonist, who gradually gains a semiotic consciousness as
he develops in the novel. The protagonist's role in the anti-moratinista
group, presented by the narrator as a prehistory of the events to follow,
reveals Gabriel's initially innocent attitude toward the sign. As the
spectator of *El sí de las niñas*, Gabriel loses his distance from the illusion
of reality that the play creates: he sees it not as artifice but as nature, as
"el colmo de la naturalidad" (the height of naturalness; 1:262). In
contrast to the protagonist, who perceives the play as a perfect imitation
of reality, the poet who leads the anti-moratinistas considers this "realism" to be a shortcoming in the dramatic work: "No se viene al teatro
para ver lo que a todas horas se ve en las calles y en casa de cada *quisque*"
(One doesn't come to the theater to see what one sees all the time in the

streets and in every person's home; 1:261), he exclaims; "¿Te parece, Gabrielito, que esto es comedia? Si no hay enredo, ni trama, ni sorpresa, ni confusiones, ni engaños, ni *quid pro quo*, ni aquello de disfrazarse un personaje para hacer creer que es otro" (Does it seem to you, Gabrielito, that this is a play? There's neither intrigue, nor plot, nor surprise, nor confusions, nor deceptions, nor quid pro quo, nor a character disguising himself to make us think he's someone else; 1:261). These characters, like Felipe Centeno and José Ido del Sagrario in the final scene of *El doctor Centeno*, exemplify two opposing ways of looking at the sign: Gabriel, who views literature as a faithful imitation of the everyday world, believes in the referentiality of language; the poet, for whom the essence of literature lies in its very artificiality (embodied in the devices of *sorpresa*, *confusiones*, and *engaños*), affirms the autonomy of language. Gabriel gradually loses his innocent vision of language as "life" itself begins to take on the qualities of the neo-romantic drama extolled by the poet.[14]

Gabriel's willing suspension of disbelief as a spectator of Moratín's play corresponds to his innocence as a spectator of yet another theatrical world, the society of the influential aristocrats, actors, and actresses, "personas muy metidas en los enredos de la Corte" (persons deeply involved in the intrigues of the Court; 1:274). These characters are performers in a theatrical production of an adaptation of *Othello* at the same time as they are participants in political and amorous intrigues in their real lives. Having just made his debut in this society, Gabriel is unable to decipher the coded language of the actors and actresses, who speak of these intrigues through the roles of the characters whose parts they play on stage. Isidoro Máiquez, Othello in the drama, refers to his jealousy in real life by declaring that he would kill "Loredano" (Juan de Mañara) if his "Edelmira" (Lesbia) should deceive him. The actors of the play, as well as the aristocratic participants in the theatrical world, are aware that they are using their fictional roles as codes through which they communicate their true situation. These codes, on the other hand, are not transparent to the uninitiated Gabriel.

14. My discussion of the protagonist's linguistic awakening is not meant to judge, either positively or negatively, his favorable response to *El sí de las niñas* at the beginning of *La corte de Carlos IV*. Many times in Galdós's works, when the romanticism/realism dichotomy (which represent, respectively, the autonomy and referentiality of language) appears to arise in a negative/positive dialectic, both of these attitudes toward literature are parodied equally. (See Alicia Andreu, "El folletín como intertexto en *Tormento*.")

Among the group of aristocrats is the Countess Amaranta, Gabriel's second employer, who initiates him into the society of the Court. The countess, well instructed in the intrigues of this world, sees history—created by the "actors" of the Court—as a labyrinth of signs that she must decode. In a central scene of the novel, "history" is written on pieces of paper that contain a coded plan of Fernando VII's conspiracy to overthrow the king. One of these papers consists of a *sainete*, whose characters are the members of the royal family; the other is also a coded message in which the prince refers to the members of his family by Gothic names. Amaranta, aware of the allegorical nature of these signs, is able to decipher them and to make sense out of the mystery that surrounds the historical event. Her talent as *decoder* of signs is directly related to her skill as *encoder* of signs. Not only does she influence the political life of the Court by fabricating intrigues, but she also manipulates Gabriel through the art of storytelling.

As Amaranta gradually awakens her servant's consciousness of language, she teaches him the art of weaving a text. She begins Gabriel's "education" by spinning the tale of the sultan and of his guard as a parable to show him that those of humble origin can rise quickly under the protection of a *señora* (lady). The story, which according to the countess comes from a book that she is reading, is in reality a literary account of the lives of Carlos IV and Manuel Godoy. It also constitutes a self-conscious reflection upon the fictional process of the adult narrator's memoirs: both the countess and Gabriel transform "history" into fiction. Yet while Gabriel disguises his narrative as truth by following the convention of the autobiographical form, Amaranta presents her narrative as a literary tale. Laying bare the fictionality of a historically based account, the countess reveals that all "history," once encoded, becomes fiction. After she narrates the second "installment" of her tale, she presents her servant with his first assignment of espionage, declaring to him that the best way to prosper in the Court is through "la intriguilla, el disimulo y el arte de conocer los corazones" (intrigue, dissimulation, and the art of reading minds; 1:315). At first, Gabriel resists the countess's efforts to teach him the language of deception: "Ya me fue imposible oír con calma una tan descarada y cínica exposición de las intrigas en que era la condesa consumada maestra y yo catecúmeno aún sin bautismo" (It was no longer possible for me to listen calmly to such an insolent and cynical exposition of the intrigues in which the countess was a consummate teacher and I an unbaptized convert; 1:317). Yet, ironically, Gabriel's metaphorical "baptism"—his linguistic awakening—has already occurred. From the first moment of his contact with Amaranta, he has begun to learn from her the art of "engañar, fingir y mentir" (deceiving, feigning, and lying; 1:350). At one moment he refuses to spy upon Amaranta's enemies for reasons of "honor"; yet at the next, he eavesdrops on his protector's conversation with the queen, thus violating this scruple. He responds to the angry countess by turning her own language back upon her: "quería empezar a instruirme cuanto antes" (I wanted to begin learning as soon as possible; 1:322).

Later in the novel, when he becomes unjustly implicated in the Fernandine conspiracy, Gabriel invents not a simple lie but a coherent narrative in order to save himself from arrest. At the end of the novel, Amaranta declares to her servant: "Me parece que has empezado bien el curso en la universidad del mundo; y, o mucho me engaño, o te bastarán pocas lecciones más para ser maestro" (It seems to me that you've well begun the course in the university of the world; and, unless I'm completely mistaken, you'll need only a few more lessons to become a master; 1:350). It is ironical, but not surprising, that the countess ultimately becomes the victim of her disciple's fabrications. In the final dialogue between the two characters, Gabriel blackmails her through the same art that she has employed previously in order to manipulate him: the art of storytelling. His tale, he says to her, is "una historia parecida a la que usía me refirió, aunque no es tan bonita" (a story similar to the one that your ladyship told me, though it isn't as pretty; 1:351). It is the story of her illicit love affair with Santorcaz. Observing her reaction of anger, the mischievous servant declares:

> Digo que desde que usía me dijo que el camino de la fortuna estaba en escuchar tras de los tapices y llevar y traer chismes de cámara en cámara, se han arreglado las cosas de tal modo, que, sin querer, estoy descubriendo secretos. (1:351)

> (I'm saying that ever since your ladyship told me that the road to fortune was in listening from behind curtains and in sending gossip back and forth from room to room, things have turned out in such a way that, without wanting to, I'm discovering secrets.)

Like Lazarillo de Tormes, who uses the very same lesson that the blind man has taught him in order to deceive his master, Gabriel ultimately turns against his "instructor" the linguistic knowledge that he has acquired from her.

Most importantly, Gabriel's apprenticeship with Amaranta gives him the linguistic consciousness necessary to write his memoirs. By teaching him the art of narrative creation, the countess also awakens the protagonist's awareness of the conventionality of literary language. As he launches his narrative in the opening pages of *Trafalgar*, the narrator, in a discursive passage, refers to the picaresque genre, comparing his story to that of Quevedo's hero: "Doy principio, pues, a mi historia como Pablos, el buscón de Segovia" (Well, I'll begin my story like Pablos, the swindler of Segovia; 1:181).[15] From the first page of the novel, the narrator is aware that his narrative is the product of a literary convention, a fiction. The protagonist himself is born out of a blank slate. Unlike other picaresque heroes, who typically begin their accounts by declaring their name and ancestry, the narrator of *Trafalgar* withholds this information from the reader throughout the first chapter: "Al hablar de mi nacimiento, no imitaré a la mayor parte de los que cuentan hechos de su propia vida, quienes empiezan nombrando su parentela . . . Yo, en esta parte, no puedo adornar mi libro con sonoros apellidos" (In speaking of my birth, I won't imitate the majority of those who narrate events in their own lives, those who begin by naming their relatives . . . I can't, in this part, adorn my book with sonorous surnames; 1:181). This omission is significant, as the narrator makes us aware that the true creator of his protagonist is not the parent who gives

15. See Emile Benveniste's useful distinction between *histoire* and *discours*. *Histoire* is a mode of utterance that characterizes the narration of past events: it refers to an impersonal, third-person narration apparently free of the narrator's presence. The discursive mode, on the other hand, is the rhetoric of the narrator: it assumes a relationship between the person of the narrator and the implied addressee (*Problems in General Linguistics*, 205–15). Galdós's *Episodios nacionales* clearly subvert the notion of history as zero-degree narration (Benveniste's *histoire*). His "historical" novels contain frequent discursive passages in which the narrator calls attention to his own rhetoric. In literary narration, discursive utterances become the mark of the self-conscious narrator who is aware of the linguistic status of his or her own narration. Roland Barthes, in "The Discourse of History," similarly debunks the notion of an objective history that "seems to tell itself" by attributing this illusion to the "reality effect": "in 'objective' history, the 'real' is never anything but an unformulated signified, sheltered behind the apparent omnipotence of the referent" (*The Rustle of Language*, 139). This displaced "signified" is the narrative configuration, the linguistic structure of historical discourse.

the character his *apellido* (surname), but the narrator himself. From the perspective of the adult writer, the protagonist is only partially created at his birth: he is truly born only when the narrative is completed. When the reader finally discovers Gabriel's first name in the second chapter of *Trafalgar*, he or she does so almost accidentally through the word of Don Alonso, the protagonist's first master. Gabriel's last name is not given to the character until the fifth book of the series (*Napoleón, en Chamartín*). After he is named viceroy of Peru, Gabriel struggles to recall his parentage in order to provide legal proof of his origin. From the "belén de mis apellidos" (bedlam of my surnames; 1:580), as Gabriel calls it, Licenciado Lobo chooses one of them, "de Araceli," to give to the character: "—¡Oh, bonitísimo! Esto de Araceli es boca de príncipes, y más de cuatro se despepitarían por llevar este nombre. Suena así como Medinaceli Coelico Metinensis, que dijo el latino. No necesito más" (Oh, how very pretty! This *Araceli* is fit for a prince, and more than four people would be raving to have this name. It sounds just like Medinaceli Coelico Metinensis, which the Latin named. I don't need more; 1:580). The name, then, reflects not the "historical" identity of the character but the identity that he gains within the context of the (not mutually exclusive) social and literary worlds to which he belongs.

It becomes increasingly evident that Gabriel invents not only himself but also the other characters in his narrative. In *La corte de Carlos IV*, the narrator reveals the process by which his beloved, Inés, comes into being as a literary creation. He portrays her as

> semejante a una de esas figuras simbólicas que, sin estar materialmente representadas en ninguna parte, se dejan ver de los ojos del alma cuando las ideas, agitándose en nuestra mente, pugnan por vestirse de formas visibles en la obscura región del cerebro. (1:264)

> (similar to one of those symbolic figures which, without being materially represented anywhere, make themselves seen by the soul's eye when ideas, stirred up in our mind, struggle to become clothed with visible forms in the obscure region of our brain.)

Inés, he suggests, exists not "materially" but as an "idea" that struggles to come into existence through the imaginative process of the writer. The narrator is aware that Inés is a product of literary conventions: "alguien encontrará digna de risa la presentación de semejante heroína y hará mil aspavientos al ver que he querido hacer una irrisoria *Beatrice* con los materiales de una modistilla" (someone will find the presentation of such a heroine deserving of laughter and will make a big fuss upon seeing that I've tried to make a ridiculous *Beatrice* out of the material of a seamstress; 1:265). As he constructs his version of the female literary archetype through his imagination, the original *modistilla* becomes a mere pretext for his inventive act.

In *El 19 de marzo y el 2 de mayo*, the narrator presents yet another self-conscious commentary on Inés's metaphorical birth in the work. When the adolescent Gabriel finds himself working as a typesetter for the *Diario de Madrid* (*Madrid Daily*), his apprenticeship in the printing business awakens his consciousness of the creative possibilities of the signs in front of him ("la caja me ofrece sus letras de plomo, que no aguardan más que mis manos para juntarse y hablar" [the box offers me its leaden letters, which await nothing other than my hands to be joined together and to speak; 1:359]) and, above all, of his power to invent Inés through these signs ("pero mi mano no conoce en los primeros momentos sino cuatro de aquellos negros signos, que al punto se reúnen para formar este solo nombre: *Inés*" [but in the first moments my hand knows only four of those black signs, which immediately join together to form this single name: *Inés*; 1:359]). The arrangement of these letters, I-N-E-S, constitutes the literal origin of the fictional character, Inés, in Gabriel's narrative. Significantly, Gabriel is a typesetter for the same newspaper through whose ads he twice finds an occupation. The *Diario* is in a sense the source of his life and adventures and, by extension, of his autobiographical account.

The figure of Inés serves an important function in Gabriel's text. A character who disappears and reappears throughout the first series of the *Episodios*, she maintains a powerful influence over the protagonist, even in her absence. She embodies an ideal of which he is in constant pursuit—an ideal that often slips away the moment that it is found. Like Gabriel, she is an orphan whose true origin remains mysterious both to the protagonist and to the reader until *Bailén*, the fourth book of the series. It is Gabriel who gives her an identity, both by discovering the "history" of her origin and by (re)writing this "history." The adolescent protagonist gradually pieces together Inés's "history" by unraveling various "texts": Juana's deathbed confession, gossip, and ultimately a written text, Santorcaz's letter to Amaranta. Gabriel unravels these texts only to weave them once again into another text, his memoirs, which contain the same story in the process of being unraveled. His literal search for Inés's identity parallels the writer's search for the character's story. The process of discovery is simultaneous with the act of narrative creation.

In *La corte de Carlos IV*, Gabriel begins his account of the courtly society by renaming the characters "la duquesa de X" (duchess of X) and "la condesa de X" (countess of X) with "nombres convencionales" (conventional names; 1:269). These linguistic designations, like his own name, are arbitrary. *Lesbia* and *Amaranta*, the names chosen for the unidentified aristocrats, originally belong to "lindas pastoras" (pretty shepherdesses; 1:269) in a work of tapestry that the narrator comes across quite accidentally while writing his memoirs. Not only the arbitrariness of these names, but also their overtly "artistic" nature call attention to the fictionality of his narrative. Immediately following the narrator's naming of Lesbia and Amaranta, he declares that language is insufficient to express their beauty: "En cuanto a su hermosura, todo lo que mi descolorida pluma pueda expresar será poco para describirlas" (As far as their beauty, anything that my colorless pen can express will be too poor to describe them; 1:269). His language, in perpetually striving to capture this imaginary ideal, becomes increasingly removed from the notion of referentiality. The written word is necessarily an autonomous fiction.

The evolution of Gabriel de Araceli's semiotic consciousness culminates in his recognition that art and life, literature and society, are alike in their creation of arbitrary systems of signs. This knowledge allows him to write his autobiography, which is in itself a form of conventional language. The narrator of *La corte de Carlos IV* reveals his consciousness of language by presenting an account of his participation in the theatrical production of *Othello* at the end of the novel. His role as actor in the play symbolizes the extent of his linguistic participation in society. Gabriel, who at the beginning of the novel is a naive spectator of *El sí de las niñas*, is now a participant in a drama that directly reflects the intrigue and deceptiveness of the Court. The adult writer, who (re)creates this event, is aware that the theater is a mirror of life: that "la intriga del drama que iba a representarse entre bastidores" (the intrigue of the drama that was about to be performed behind the scenes) has begun to imitate art, "el [drama] comenzado sobre las tablas y ante el público" (the drama begun on the stage in front of the public; 1:337). Gabriel is the spectator of the "drama entre bastidores." He eavesdrops on the conversation between Isidoro and Lesbia, who recognize the link between their roles on stage as Othello and Edelmira and off stage in their real lives. Between acts, Isidoro admits that he has come to identify completely with Othello's jealousy; Lesbia, in turn, exclaims to Isidoro: "No eres Isidoro, eres Otelo en persona" (You aren't Isidoro, you're Othello in person; 1:340). Soon the narrator himself begins to refer consistently to Isidoro as "el moro" (the Moor) even when the actor is off the stage.

Gabriel's own role as Pésaro (Iago) is suggestive. In the original play by Shakespeare, tragedy is a direct result of the villain's linguistic talent: Iago deceives Othello by fabricating a narrative and, finally, by presenting to the Moor a false sign of his wife's infidelity. Significantly, this sign, a handkerchief in Shakespeare's drama, has been replaced by a letter in this twice-translated version of the play.[16] In the final act of the play, Pepa substitutes for the fictional letter a real one (written by Lesbia), which becomes a proof of Lesbia's infidelity to Isidoro in real life. It is therefore a written text that makes possible the fusion of reality and fiction at the end of the play. This text, moreover, simultaneously deceives and reveals the truth. Within the context of the play, the letter is a false sign of Edelmira/Desdemona's infidelity; in "life," however, it exposes the truth of Lesbia's infidelity. The meaning of this text, like that of all texts, is a direct function of the context that governs its interpretation. The *mise en abyme* technique—the text (the letter) within the text (the twice-translated *Othello*) within the text (Gabriel's *memoirs*)—which serves as a self-conscious commentary on the signifying process itself, forces the reader to recognize the conventionality of all notions of truth and fictionality. Gabriel/Pésaro's act of delivering the fatal letter to Isidoro/Otelo in the final scene of the play causes Isidoro to lose distance from his role. In his jealous anger, he nearly kills the terrified Lesbia, who has deceived him in real life. Although Gabriel becomes fully aware of the role that Pepa has staged for him only at the end of the drama, the part that he plays within the theatrical representation symbolizes his increasing consciousness of the deceptive sign and of the language of deception.

After he leaves Amaranta's service at the end of *La corte de Carlos IV*,

16. The translated version of Shakespeare's work may be seen as a metaphor for the narrator's historical/autobiographical writing. Translation suggests a process of linguistic transformation. It is, in a literal sense, a "taking beyond" (from the Latin *trans* [across/beyond] and *latus* [carried]) of the original. Gabriel's memoirs, a "translation" of social and personal history, necessarily involve an act of creation. His discourse thus replaces the original reality that it purports to represent.

Gabriel stages his own fictions, using lessons that he has learned in the Court. In *Napoleón, en Chamartín*, Gabriel and his former employer become cast as rivals in the art of fiction-making. The countess, with her "extremada habilidad artística" (consummate artistic skill; 1:633), stages an intricate drama through which she tries to manipulate the fates of Gabriel and her daughter Inés. At the same time as she helps him to escape from French-occupied Madrid by disguising him in her cousin's clothing, she invents an intricate lie by which she tries to convince Inés of her former servant's death. "Lo que más le ha convencido fue el artificio verdaderamente teatral que puse en práctica para hacérselo creer" (What convinced her the most was the truly theatrical artifice that I put into practice to make her believe it; 1:633), she declares, referring to her talent as actress in her drama. Her linguistic skill in her "artificio teatral" is inseparable from her ability to manipulate the social sign, as reflected in the fusion of theater and society. Gabriel, in imitation of Amaranta, produces his representation. Rather than conforming to the part that the countess has assigned him in her fiction, he "writes" his own role in the drama with a full consciousness of its conventions. Not only does he return to the palace disguised as the duke of Arion, but he also acts out the role of the duke, using his linguistic talent. By this time, he has learned to manipulate the discourse of the Court well enough to deceive its personages temporarily. Upon discovering Gabriel's art, Amaranta, outwitted by him once again, exclaims to him: "Hipócrita, ¿dónde has aprendido a fingir?" (Hypocrite, where did you learn to pretend?; 1:653). The irony of these words is apparent, since it is the countess who has given him lessons in "engaños y ficciones" (deception and falsehood; 1:633) throughout his apprenticeship in the Court. His relationship to his former employer is perpetually ironic: the language that he has learned originally from her allows him to manipulate her, to subvert her fictions, and ultimately to (re)create her in his narrative account.

   The art of role-playing, which Gabriel gradually masters throughout the first series, becomes increasingly dependent on a specifically literary consciousness. In *Cádiz*, society, contained in the microcosm of the Rumblar home, emerges as a stage for the literary fictions of Gabriel and other characters. Upon entering the Rumblar home, where Inés is held against her will, Gabriel senses the theatricality of "esta morada del disimulo y la mentira" (this abode of dissimulation and lies; 1:879), whose *tertulias* (social gatherings) he characterizes as "una completa representación de teatro" (a complete theatrical performance; 1:880).

One of the principal actors on this stage is the Englishman Lord Gray. A prototypical romantic hero, he comes to Spain in search of the unconventional, the sublime, and the imaginative, and he steps into the Spain that he has envisioned through his reading of literature. He seduces Asunción, whose "mysticism" intrigues him, sees La Celestina in his go-between ("Admirable tipo que hace revivir a mi lado la incomparable tragicomedia de Rodrigo Cota y Fernando de Rojas" [Admirable character who brings back to life, right by my side, the incomparable tragicomedy of Rodrigo Cota and Fernando de Rojas; 1:915]), and, finally, recognizes Don Quixote in Gabriel, who seeks justice for the offended woman. As in *Don Quixote*, the literary imagination becomes contagious. In order to gain entrance into the Rumblar home, Gabriel plays the role of the Spanish mystic and at the same time defends the reactionary and absolutist values of the clergy. His role is never questioned in the Rumblar household, not only because he has mastered the art of role-playing, but also because the theatricality of life within the aristocratic society makes it impossible for anyone to distinguish truth from lie, reality from literature. Gabriel's literary consciousness also allows him to step into the role of Don Quixote at the end of the novel. Following the example of the knight-errant, he determines to avenge Asunción's dishonor by challenging her seducer to a duel. His sense of justice not only leads him to identify with Cervantes's hero, but also to imitate his language. At one point in his dialogue with Lord Gray, he asserts, "Yo soy quien soy" (I am who I am; 1:950), echoing Don Quixote's ironic affirmation of his self-identity. Gabriel, like Don Quixote, is aware that he is representing a role in a world that he has transformed through his knowledge of literature. His prophetic words, "Después de las burlas pueden venir las veras" (After the joke comes the truth; 1:950), which again evoke Cervantes's text, reveal the protagonist's awareness of the fine line that separates fiction from reality. The scene of the duel is a rewriting of the episode in the second part of *Don Quixote* in which the knight-errant upsets Sansón Carrasco's fiction by defeating him in a duel that the Bachiller has staged. The outcome of the joint "fiction" of Gabriel and Lord Gray is predictable: the protagonist defeats his opponent, who dies in the battle. "Las burlas" have become "las veras" for both characters.

The gap between the adult narrator and the young protagonist gradually diminishes as the latter becomes increasingly self-conscious of his participation in a literary world. By the last book of the first series, the character is more aware than ever that his entire existence is a function of the all-pervasive world of literature about him. In *La batalla de los Arapiles*, the quixotic Miss Fly, who revives the "romantic" Spain that Lord Gray has envisioned in *Cádiz*, imposes the world of literature on Gabriel's life. Through her "monomanía literaria" (literary mono-mania; 2:43), she transforms him into the *caballero enamorado* (lovestruck knight) of her books of chivalry and adopts the language of chivalry, addressing the protagonist as "vos" (thou) and referring to Inés as "vuestra dama" (your ladyship; 2:34). Gabriel, rather than fleeing from this world of literature, willingly steps into the role that Miss Fly has cast for him in the world of knights-errant, enchanters, and damsels in distress. Recognizing the poet in himself, he reinvents his life through language. As the narrator explains, "Todos somos algo poetas, y es muy dulce embellecer la propia vida, y muy natural regocijarnos con este embellecimiento, aun sabiendo que la transformación es obra nuestra" (We all have the poet in us, and it's pleasing to embellish our own lives, and very natural to delight in this embellishment, even knowing that the transformation is our own work; 2:34). In accordance with the conven-tions of the romances of chivalry, Gabriel recreates the events of his life—his pursuit of Inés, whom Santorcaz has abducted and disguised as a "comiquilla" (little actress)—as a tale of a knight in search of his beloved woman ("[una dama] hermosísima y principal" [a very beau-tiful and illustrious lady]), whom an enchanter has transfigured into a "vulgar comiquilla" (2:34). Miss Fly recognizes the conventionality of the protagonist's tale by exclaiming, "Veo que leéis libros de caba-llerías" (I see that you read books of chivalry; 2:34), and by affirming that the world of the books of chivalry cannot exist outside the imagina-tion. By the same token, when she discovers that Gabriel's story is based on "life," she declares that it is "tan hermoso que no parece real" (so beautiful that it doesn't seem real; 2:43). Miss Fly's distinction between life and literature becomes ironic as she begins to confuse the two worlds. Upon seeing the extraordinary in life, she exclaims with sur-prise, "Eso sí que no estaba escrito en mis libros" (Now that, certainly, wasn't written in my books; 2:69).[17] Gabriel must remind the English-

17. In his "Observaciones sobre la novela contemporánea en España," Galdós speaks of the apparent paradox by which the same readers who are bewildered by the invasion of the "novelistic" into real life can fall easily into the trap of illusionist art, believing that the novelistic is life: "Cuando vemos un acontecimiento extraor-dinariamente anómalo y singular, decimos que *parece cosa de novela*; y cuando tro-pezamos con algún individuo extremadamente raro, le llamamos *héroe de novela*, y nos

woman of the fine line that separates literature from life:

> Usted cree que todos los lances de amor y de aventura han de pasar en el mundo conforme a lo que ha leído en las novelas, en los romances, en las obras de los grandes poetas y escritores, y no advierte que las cosas extrañas y dramáticas suelen verse antes en la vida real que en los libros, llenos de ficciones convencionales y que se reproducen unas a otras. (2:69)

> (You believe that all episodes of love and adventure have to happen in the world according to what you've read in novels, in ballads, in the works of great poets and writers, and you don't notice that strange and dramatic things are often more likely to be seen in real life than in books filled with conventional fictions that give rise to one another.)

Life imitates art, as the narrative of Gabriel's life unfolds in accordance with the conventions of the chivalric romance. His role as hero of Miss Fly's (and his own) romance ultimately becomes inseparable from his real identity. In the final scene of the novel, he even courts Inés by imitating the chivalric language that he has learned from the Englishwoman. The narratives that the character creates within the larger narrative reflect the process of autobiographical writing through which the narrator ultimately converts himself into a text. The protagonist's words to Miss Fly, "Resignémonos a ser libro de texto" (Let's resign ourselves to being textbooks; 2:33), which reveal his awareness of himself as a text to be read by others, anticipate his textual self-transformation through the writing of his memoirs.

---

reímos de él porque se nos presenta con toda la extrañeza e inusitada forma con que le hemos visto en aquellos extravagantes libros. En cambio, cuando leemos las admirables obras de arte que produjo Cervantes y hoy hace Carlos Dickens, decimos: '¡Qué verdadero es esto! Parece cosa de la vida. Tal o cual personaje, parece que le hemos conocido'" (When we see an extraordinarily anomalous and singular event, we say that it *seems to be out of a novel*; and when we run into some extremely strange individual, we call him *hero of a novel*, and we laugh at him because he is presented to us with all the strangeness and unusual form with which we've seen him in those extravagant books. In contrast, when we read the admirable works of art that Cervantes produced or that Charles Dickens writes today, we say: "How true this is! It seems like life. Such or such character, it seems like we've met him") (*Ensayos*, 118–19). Galdós suggests that these two phenomena are two sides of the same coin, since to see the "novelistic" elements in life in the first place presumes a belief in the existence of a "mundo de novela" (novelistic world).

The adult narrator constantly plays with the opposition that underlies his vision of language: on the one hand, he affirms his belief in the
referentiality of language; on the other, he asserts the autonomy of
language. In the context of the *Episodios nacionales*, the conflict between
these two theories of language can be translated into the tension between the narrator's dual role as chronicler of history and as inventor of
fictions. His role as "historian" in the first series, however, is undermined by his consciousness of his self-creative act. In a historical text,
any suggestion of the autonomy of language necessarily subverts the
validity of its fundamental project: the representation of a historical
truth. Once the protagonist becomes aware of his textuality, the narrator can no longer affirm the historicity of all else embraced by the
same text. As Ricardo Gullón writes: "Lo histórico y lo ficticio están
tejidos en la novela con la misma clase de fibra" (The historical and the
fictional are woven in the novel with the same kind of thread).[18] Once
historical figures and events are placed within a fictional framework,
they become indistinguishable from their purely literary counterparts.

The narrator of the first series often calls attention to the "historicity" of his account, only to ironize his affirmation. In *Bailén*, for
example, he interrupts his story (*histoire*) to explain why he has empha-
sized the words of one of the characters: "He subrayado estas palabras,
porque son puntualmente históricas; constan en papeles impresos de
aquel tiempo, que puedo mostrar al que verlos desee" (I've underlined
these words, because they're historically accurate; they're recorded in
printed papers of that time, which I can show to anyone who wishes to
see them; 1:482). According to the narrator's claim, he has underscored
these words in order to show us that he has transcribed them directly
from a historical source. In the next line, however, he indicates paren-
thetically that these words do not belong to the character to whom he has
attributed them: "(pues no fue doña María, y el atribuirlo a ésta es de
mi exclusiva responsabilidad)" [(well it wasn't Doña María, attributing
it to her is my exclusive responsibility); 1:482]. This "aside" not only
undermines the narrator's original assertion of the historicity of his
account, but also serves as a reminder of his authorial power over his
narrative. Moreover, he alleges the historicity of the character's words
by referring not to the events themselves but to another textual source:
in this way, Gabriel lays bare the linguistic nature of his historical
writing. His text, rather than being the representation of an absolute
historical truth, is a rewriting of another text.

18. "La historia como materia novelable," 23.

In the opening pages of *Napoleón, en Chamartín*, the adult narrator
makes his pretensions to historical accuracy ironic by parodying the
conventions of historical documentation. He begins the novel with a
portrayal of the dissipated don Diego de Rumblar:

> Aquí tenía principio, según opinión de los sesudos autores que se han
> ocupado de don Diego de Rumblar, la verdadera existencia de aquel
> insigne rapazuelo, y también es cierto que todos los cronistas, si bien
> desacordes en algunos pormenores de estas escandalosas aventuras,
> están conformes en afirmar que siempre le acompañaba el supradicho
> Mañara, y que casi nunca dejaban de visitar a una altísima dama, la
> cual lo era sin duda por vivir en un tercer piso de la calle de la Pasión, y
> tenía por nombre *la Zaina* o *la Zunga*, pues en este punto existe una
> lamentable discordancia entre autores, cronistas, historiógrafos y demás
> graves personas que de las hazañas de tan famosa hembra han tratado.
> (1:547)

(According to the opinion of the wise authors who've concerned themselves with Don Diego de Rumblar, here was the beginning of the true
existence of that illustrious street urchin, and it's also true that all the
chroniclers, even if they're in complete disagreement about some details
of these scandalous adventures, agree in affirming that the above-men-
tioned Mañara always accompanied him, and that they never failed to
visit a very high lady, which she doubtlessly was, due to the fact that she
lived on the third floor of Passion Street, and she was called *la Zaina* or *la
Zunga*, for on this point there exists a lamentable disagreement among
authors, chroniclers, historiographers, and other important persons
who've dealt with the deeds of such a renowned female.)

The narrator's language is completely playful: he uses ironic epithets
("insigne rapazuelo"), puns ("altísima dama, la cual lo era sin duda por
vivir en un tercer piso de la calle de la Pasión"), and bathos (the juxtaposition of the epithet *famosa* with the derogatory *hembra*). The entire
passage, moreover, echoes the language of the narrator of *Don Quixote*,
who refers equally ironically to the historical sources from which he
draws his "verdadera historia" (true story). The narrator, by calling
attention to the irony of his rhetoric, undercuts any claim that he might
make to the historicity of his account. Significantly, after he pretends to
struggle with the question of the woman's "true" name, he exercises his
authorial freedom by choosing her name: "yo me decido a llamarla
siempre *la Zaina*" (I've decided always to call her *la Zaina*; 1:547).

At the end point of his narrative, the narrator calls attention to an accusation that could undermine the historicity of his writing. He playfully suggests, in the concluding pages of *La batalla de los Arapiles*, the possibility that Miss Fly has never existed: "Muchas personas que anteriormente me han oído contar esto, sostienen que jamás ha existido miss Fly; que toda esta parte de mi historia es una invención mía para recrearme a mí propio y entretener a los demás" (Many people who've previously heard me recount this, claim that Miss Fly never existed, that this entire part of my story is an invention of mine in order to amuse myself and to entertain others; 2:137). Yet at no time does he directly negate the fictionality of Miss Fly or affirm her existence in the real world. He responds, "pero ¿no debe creerse ciegamente la palabra de un hombre honrado?" (but, shouldn't the word of an honorable man be blindly trusted?; 2:137), suggesting not that the accusation is untrue but that the reader should suspend his or her disbelief and blindly accept the word of the narrator. Moreover, Gabriel's attempt to attest to his credibility by presenting himself as "un hombre honrado" is also ironic, since "honor," in the context of his evolution, represents not an absolute quality of moral worth, but the ability to manipulate language. The narrator's subsequent words, "Por ventura, quien de tanta rectitud dio pruebas, ¿será capaz ahora de obscurecer su reputación con ficciones absurdas, con fábricas de la imaginación que no tengan por base y fundamento la misma verdad, hija de Dios?" (Do you think, perchance, that a person who's given proof of such rectitude will now be capable of tarnishing his reputation with absurd fictions, with imaginary fabrications which do not have truth itself, the child of God, as their base and foundation?; 2:137), constitute more than a simple rhetorical question. Through the very act of posing this question, he calls attention to the possibility that his narrative may be other than the representation of a historical truth. Finally, the name *Miss Fly* calls attention to itself as a sign of fictionality. The reader cannot but see the "natural" affinity between the impertinent and meddling Miss Fly (often referred to as *Mosquita* (little fly), *Mariposa* (butterfly), or *Pajarita* (little bird) by Gabriel and the other characters) and her name. This "natural relation of names and essences" becomes, once again, a sign of the literary function.[19]

In Galdós's *Episodios nacionales*, historical writing always involves the process of linguistic transformation, as exemplified in Gabriel's self-

19. Barthes, *New Critical Essays*, 67–68.

conscious conversion of personal and national history into a literary text. Throughout the first series, many other characters also engage in the making of history, whether by simply interpreting the events around them or by actually composing a written "historical" text. As each character, or each member of society, interprets, reinvents, and fictionalizes the historical event, the notion of historical accuracy eventually dissipates. In *Trafalgar*, the pathological liar, José María Malespina, invents his version of history by transforming himself into a hero of the battle of Trafalgar. As the narrator claims, Malespina's account is none other than "una novela de heroísmo" (a novel of heroism; 1:252). In *La corte de Carlos IV*, each member of society interprets Fernando VII's letters in his or her own way in an attempt to understand the truth behind the prince's conspiracy to overthrow his father. These letters, which contain the prince's supposed apology to the king for his role in the plot, are transcribed in *La Gaceta de Madrid* (*The Gazette of Madrid*) along with a royal decree. The apparent truth contained in these letters, however, is cast into doubt by those who claim that Godoy, in an attempt to humiliate the prince, has forced him to invent a text. In *Gerona*, Pablo de Nomdedeu (whose Catalan name, translated as "Name of God," suggests his status as yet another creator figure) constructs elaborate texts in order to protect his deaf and invalid daughter from the realities of the war that surrounds them. These texts, which take the form of letters to his daughter, contain a curious mixture of history and fiction: Nomdedeu, who artfully constructs a fictional account of the siege of Gerona, at the same time cites historical figures, events, and statistics in order to render his account verisimilar. *Gerona*, the only novel of the first series that Gabriel does not directly narrate, is nevertheless his rewriting of Andresillo Marijuán's account of the siege: Gabriel admits to giving "uniformity" to his memoirs by modifying his friend's style and by adding other elements to his narration. History therefore comes to the reader twice mediated. At the end of *La batalla de los Arapiles*, Amaranta, through her epistolary mania, transforms Gabriel into a holder of successively higher military titles.

The narrator assimilates these texts, each of which contains a separate version of history, into a single narrative. This narrative, which consists of the entire first series of the *Episodios*, lays bare the fictional nature of history-making by dramatizing the awakening of the narrator's consciousness of the linguistic sign. It is precisely his new semiotic consciousness that allows the mature Gabriel to transform himself and his historical context textually. Benveniste has defined the privileged place of language among all sign systems as its "metalinguistic faculty," its capacity to interpret other systems.[20] History, in Gabriel's text, is a labyrinth of individual and social fictions, all arbitrary systems of signs. In writing his memoirs, the narrator of the first series uses language in order to interpret and to lay bare the various "fictions" in the world of the protagonist. Gabriel's autobiographical narrative thus seems to show us that history is no more than a pre-text for the narrator's fictionalizations. Our recognition of the fictionality of the narrative account does not negate the historical illusion created within the world of the novel. We can still read the *Episodios nacionales* to learn about the historical events of nineteenth-century Spain, but at the same time we are reminded, through the novels' self-conscious presentation of history, that our very knowledge of these events is mediated by language.

The linguistic self-consciousness in the *Episodios nacionales* indicates that these novels share the semiotic preoccupations of the *Novelas españolas contemporáneas*. The *Episodios* and the *Novelas españolas contemporáneas* alike dramatize the tension between historical representation and fictional creation, between mimesis and metafiction. By linking the course of national history and the structure of events in the characters' lives, both sets of novels produce the illusion that history is unfolding before our eyes.[21] At the same time, the characters' manipulation and creation of signs call attention to the status of literature as a linguistically and semiotically self-reflective artifact. In the end, Galdós's *Episodios* show us that "truth" in the historical novel lies in the process of its self-definition, a process that involves, simultaneously, the creation of a mimetic convention and the laying bare of that convention.

20. "The Semiology of Language," 243.

21. In Part 3 of *Fortunata y Jacinta*, for example, the restoration of order in the marriage of Jacinta and Juanito Santa Cruz occurs simultaneously with the restoration of Alfonso XII's monarchy. As Spain's First Republic falls, Juanito Santa Cruz resolves to abandon his illicit love affair in order to embrace the orderly life, represented by the metaphor of the monarchy. See Bly, *Galdós's Novel of the Historical Imagination*, for a more extensive discussion of Galdós's novels as an allegory of national history.

Conclusion

L'écriture réaliste est loin d'être neutre, elle est au contraire chargée des signes les plus spectaculaires de la fabrication.

—Roland Barthes

(Realist writing is far from being neutral; it is, on the contrary, charged with the most spectacular signs of fabrication.)

The only realism in art is of the imagination.

—William Carlos Williams, *Spring and All*

The theoretical framework of my study implies a view of the writer as a semiotician who carefully constructs a novelistic world in which each structure, each textual fragment, forms a microcosm of the whole. At the same time, we have seen that this whole—the semiotic system of the Galdosian text—represents not a unity but a multiplicity of contradictory voices and visions. As Bakhtin claims in his famous study of novelistic dialogism, "the language of a novel is the system of its 'languages.'"[1] The interrelationship between various "languages" in Galdós's novels is infinitely complex, whether this language belongs to characters or to narrators, to an individual or to society, to the marginalized or to the integrated, to the mad or to the sane. Each system within the text reflects the nature of the whole without any single one subordinating the others. Each constitutes a self-sufficient social, historical, existential, or fictional world with which the reader can identify, and each is also a subversion of this world. Clearly, one measure of the greatness of Gal-

---

1. "Discourse in the Novel," 262. Alicia Andreu's *Modelos dialógicos en la narrativa de Benito Pérez Galdós* appeared shortly before I reviewed the proofs for the present study. In her book, Andreu bases her readings of five representative novels of Galdós on Bakhtinian theory, in particular on the Russian critic's notion of "dialogism." Andreu demonstrates that the Galdosian text constitutes a dialogue of multiple discursive voices and (inter)texts—a dialogue which has led to the creation of a "nueva narrativa galdosiana" (new Galdosian narrative), characterized by "ambigüedad y ambivalencia" (ambiguity and ambivalence) (xvi).

dós's works lies in the intricacy of his semiotic system, reflected in the tensions embedded in every level of the textual structure.

The complexity of linguistic and semiotic self-consciousness in Galdós's works demands that we question the established opposition between twentieth-century avant-garde fiction and the works of nineteenth-century realism. Even Galdós's contemporary Henry James, who in his own fiction obsessively dramatizes the semiotic adventure, relegates nineteenth-century fiction to a strictly representational role. In his famous essay "The Art of Fiction," he criticizes the novel's use of frame-breaking techniques as "a betrayal of a sacred office." For James, an exposure of the novel's artifice represents an apology for its fictionality, for its nature as "make-believe."[2] This kind of thinking by a prominent writer has perhaps led to a more widespread condemnation, by writers and critics alike, of literary self-reflexivity in nineteenth-century novels. In the view of many twentieth-century authors, the realist novel represents a replete sign or, to borrow Barthes's term, a "readerly" text, against which they are deliberately reacting.[3] They characterize their own texts, on the other hand, as subversive, playful, and even antirealist. (The Spanish *noventayochistas'* critique of Galdós and, to use a more international example, Julio Cortázar's parody of *Lo prohibido* in *Rayuela* illustrate the case in point.) The characteristics that many have attributed to these two supposedly separate categories of texts have become hierarchized, that is, charged with value: twentieth-century texts are commonly privileged over nineteenth-century works as a more interesting space for critical exploration. Such an attitude underlies, for example, Jonathan Culler's discussion of the possibilities of structuralist criticism:

> When reading a nineteenth-century novel we speed up and slow down, and the rhythm of our reading is a recognition of structure: we can pass quickly through those descriptions and conversations whose functions identify; we wait for something more important, at which point we slow down. If we reversed this rhythm we would no doubt become bored. With a modern text that we cannot organize as the adventures of a character, we cannot skip and modulate our speed in the same way without encountering opacity and boredom; we must read more slowly,

2. "The Art of Fiction," 662.
3. *S/Z*, 4.

savouring the drama of the sentence, exploring local indeterminacies, and working out the general project which they promote or resist.

Despite their place within nineteenth-century realism, Galdós's novels present at every turn "the adventures of meaning," which Culler associates principally with the avant-garde tradition.[4] These texts point as much to the conditions of meaning as to the meaning itself. The example of Galdós has shown that the self-critique that modernists have attributed almost exclusively to twentieth-century fiction and to a few "exceptional" works of previous centuries (such as *Don Quijote* and *Tristram Shandy*) is also a notable feature of the nineteenth-century novel.

It is not sufficient, however, simply to affirm the existence of self-consciousness in the realist tradition. A more interesting problem is the mutual dependence between mimesis and metafiction, between referentiality and self-referentiality. As Linda Hutcheon observes, "metafiction is still fiction, despite the shift in focus of narration from the product it presents to the process it is. Auto-representation is still representation."[5] In Galdós's novels, we have seen that the text is the space in which theories of fiction and of language are played out: the boundary between fiction and theory is thus eliminated. More specifically, the text embodies implicit and explicit commentaries on the conventions of realism and of referentiality, central theoretical preoccupations in Galdós's works.

In many nineteenth-century works, realism paradoxically becomes the sign of the novel's self-consciousness. Implicit in the traditional notion of realism is the desire to deny the conventionality of literary discourse by concealing or even destroying narrative artifice. Yet in its attempt to mask the signs of literary convention, realist discourse often transforms the idea of conventionality into a theoretical problem. Galdós's novels dramatize precisely this paradox. Many of his works parody and subvert any notion of nature (or of "raw material" in art) on several levels: on the stylistic level (in the narrator's use of parodic and playful language), on the level of the narrator's discourse (exemplified by self-conscious narratorial interventions and by frame-breaking techniques), and on the allegorical level (embodied in the character's trajectory as interpreter and creator of signs). The exchange between Ponce and

4. *Structuralist Poetics*, 263, 262.
5. *Narcissistic Narrative*, 39.

Ballester in Fortunata's funeral scene (see Chapter 2 above), for example, becomes an emblem for the process of the novel in its entirety.[6] Through this dialogue, the narrator suggests that Galdós's realism, far from being a naive copy of life itself, is "la vulgaridad de la vida" (the vulgarity of life), the raw material of life, artistically recreated into "materia estética" (aesthetic material; 2:977). Máximo Manso's failure to transform Irene and Manolo Peña (whom the narrator presents as "un perfecto trozo del mármol más fino para labrar una estatua" [a perfect slab of the finest marble to create a statue; 1:1193]) into authentic signs mirrors within the novel's "inner" frame the subversion of the mimetic convention operative on the level of the narrator's text (the "outer" frame). We have seen that such interior texts, spoken and written, fabricated by narrators and characters alike, abound in Galdós's novels. The example of Felipe Centeno shows that the semiotic adventures of some interior readers can form an allegory of Galdosian realism: the character's impossible quest for truth self-consciously parallels the process by which the novel unmasks the notion of the natural sign. Perhaps the unmasking of the referential illusion is most explicit in *La incógnita*, in which the deliberately playful style of the first-person narrator undermines his own claim to the mimetic nature of his language. Galdós's creations teach us that, ultimately, literature can do no more than to affirm its "inevitably unrealistic status."[7]

In "Writing and the Novel," Barthes suggests that even the most perfect realism, exemplified in the "ordered" world of Flaubert's novels, cannot escape self-consciousness.[8] For Barthes, the *passé simple* and the third-person narrator, two devices that are designed to produce pure illusion in the realist novel, become signs of creation by virtue of their artificiality. The exaggeration of conventions and the attempt to destroy them are thus mutually related and many times inseparable. Galdós's obsession with realism likewise finds expression in his play with the signs of fabrication. While the self-consciousness of Flaubert's realism (and that of his Spanish counterpart Clarín) is more limited in scope, Galdós's play with the artifices of fiction extends to every sphere of his texts. The characters of both Flaubert's *Madame Bovary* and Clarín's *La*

6. See Hazel Gold's "Problems of Closure in *Fortunata y Jacinta*" for a more extensive discussion of the theory of Galdosian fiction contained in the final chapter of the novel.

7. Barthes, *Critical Essays*, 267.

8. *Writing Degree Zero*, 29–40.

Regenta undoubtedly participate in the acts of reading and creation. Yet the overall narrative consistency produced by the free indirect style often counters the creation of multiple textual levels that can call the mimetic project of the novel into question in a profound way. Although stylistic craft, taken to an extreme, can lead to the unmasking of illusionist art, as Barthes claims, the novels of Flaubert and Clarín, exemplary of such craft, present their self-critique primarily on the thematic rather than on the narratorial level. In contrast, the Galdosian narrator explicitly calls attention to his narrative art both by donning various masks at once and by constantly yielding his discourse to countless other interior narrators. Galdós's novels not only present an endless cast of characters engaged in semiotic reflection, but also explicitly use frame-breaking techniques, allowing characters and narrators alike to comment on the literary and linguistic nature of the texts in which they appear. Manso's account of his fictional birth and death in *El amigo Manso*, the literary disquisitions of Felipe and José Ido del Sagrario in the "frames" of *El doctor Centeno* and *Tormento*, and the exchange between Ponce and Ballester in the final chapter of *Fortunata y Jacinta*, to name only a few examples, all become overt signs of artistic creation.

The paradox of modernism, Barthes continues, is that it "begins with the search for a Literature which is no longer possible."[9] The coexistence of apparently contradictory tendencies in Galdós's novels thus marks the emergence of a modern consciousness in the nineteenth-century novel. In this light, Galdós can be seen as a transitional figure between the highly codified, "pure" realism (exemplified by Flaubert and Clarín) and the avant-garde literary tradition of the twentieth century, in which the works themselves intentionally subvert the pretense of traditional realism in a most radical way. As Borges (and T. S. Eliot before him) has affirmed, each work, and each tradition, creates its own precursors.[10] The overtly self-flaunting techniques of modern fiction have allowed the present-day reader to gain a greater consciousness of the metafictionality implicit in all literature, including realist novels. The reader learns to unmask the signs of realism in the same way in which modernist (or post-modernist) fiction unmasks itself. The perspectives that the works of our contemporaries suggest can thus open new ways of approaching older texts. Galdós's fiction, exemplary within the realist tradition for its explicit self-consciousness, can similarly pro-

9. Ibid., 38.
10. "Kafka y sus precursores," 109.

vide a model for studying other works of nineteenth-century realism as linguistically and semiotically self-reflective texts. The reexamination of nineteenth-century fiction from this new perspective will undoubtedly enrich our understanding not only of these works, but of modern literature, which continues to transform itself through its never-ending dialogue with realist literature.

Works Cited

Alas, Leopoldo (Clarín). *Galdós*. Madrid: Renacimiento, 1912.

Alter, Robert. *Partial Magic: The Novel as a Self-Conscious Genre*. Berkeley: University of California Press, 1978.

Altman, Janet. *Epistolarity: Approaches to a Form*. Columbus: Ohio State University Press, 1982.

Anderson, Farris. "Ellipsis and Space in *Tristana*." *Anales Galdosianos* 20 (1985): 61–76.

Andreu, Alicia. "El folletín como intertexto en *Tormento*." *Anales Galdosianos* 17 (1982): 55–61.

———. *Galdós y la literatura popular*. Madrid: Sociedad General Española de Librería, 1982.

———. *Modelos dialógicos en la narrativa de Benito Pérez Galdós*. Philadelphia: John Benjamins Publishing Company, 1989.

Aristotle. *Poetics*. Translated by Gerald F. Else. Ann Arbor: University of Michigan Press, 1970.

Auerbach, Erich. *Mimesis: The Representation of Reality in Western Literature*. Princeton: Princeton University Press, 1953.

Ayala, Francisco. "Galdós entre el lector y los personajes." *Anales Galdosianos* 5 (1970): 5–13.

Bakhtin, Mikhail M. "Discourse in the Novel." In *The Dialogic Imagination*, translated by Caryl Emerson and Michael Holquist, 259–422. Austin: University of Texas Press, 1982.

Barthes, Roland. *Critical Essays*. Translated by Richard Howard. Evanston: Northwestern University Press, 1972.

———. *Image-Music-Text*. Translated by Stephen Heath. New York: Hill and Wang, 1977.

———. *Mythologies*. Translated by Annette Lavers. New York: Hill and Wang, 1972.

———. *New Critical Essays*. Translated by Richard Howard. New York: Hill and Wang, 1986.

———. *The Rustle of Language*. Translated by Richard Howard. New York: Hill and Wang, 1986.

———. *S/Z*. Translated by Richard Miller. New York: Hill and Wang, 1974.

———. *Writing Degree Zero*. Translated by Annette Lavers and Colin Smith. New York: Hill and Wang, 1984.

Benveniste, Emile. *Problems in General Linguistics*. Translated by Mary Elizabeth Meek. Coral Gables: University of Miami Press, 1971.

―――. "The Semiology of Language." In *Semiotics: An Introductory Anthology*, edited by Robert E. Innis, 226–46. Bloomington: Indiana University Press, 1985.

Bly, Peter A. *Galdós's Novel of the Historical Imagination*. Liverpool Monographs in Hispanic Studies, 2. Liverpool: Francis Cairns, 1983.

Bonet, Laureano. *De Galdós a Robbe-Grillet*. Madrid: Taurus, 1972.

Borges, Jorge Luis. "Kafka y sus precursores." In *Otras inquisiciones*, 107–9. Madrid: Alianza, 1985.

Bosch, Rafael. "Galdós y la teoría de la novela de Lukács." *Anales Galdosianos* 2 (1967): 169–84.

Boyd, Michael. *The Reflexive Novel: Fiction as Critique*. Lewisburg, Pa.: Bucknell University Press, 1983.

Burke, Kenneth. *The Rhetoric of Religion: Studies in Logology*. Berkeley: University of California Press, 1961.

Casalduero, Joaquín. *Vida y obra de Galdós*. 4th ed. Madrid: Editorial Gredos, 1974.

Cervantes Saavedra, Miguel de. *El ingenioso hidalgo Don Quijote de la Mancha*. 2 vols. Edited by Luis Murillo. Madrid: Editorial Castalia, 1978.

Chamberlin, Vernon A. "Poor Maxi's Windmill: Aquatic Symbolism in *Fortunata y Jacinta*." *Hispanic Review* 50 (1982): 427–37.

Correa, Gustavo. "Pérez Galdós y la tradición calderoniana." *Cuadernos Hispanoamericanos* 250–52 (1970–1971): 227–30.

―――. *Realidad, ficción y símbolo en las novelas de Pérez Galdós*. Bogotá: Instituto Caro y Cuervo, 1967.

Culler, Jonathan. Foreword. In *The Poetics of Prose*, by Tzvetan Todorov, translated by Richard Howard, 7–13. Ithaca: Cornell University Press, 1977.

―――. *Structuralist Poetics*. Ithaca: Cornell University Press, 1975.

Dante Alighieri. *Inferno*. Translated by John D. Sinclair. New York: Oxford University Press, 1980.

Dendle, Brian J. *Galdós: The Early Historical Novels*. Columbia: University of Missouri Press, 1986.

Derrida, Jacques. *Of Grammatology*. Translated by Gayatri Spivak. Baltimore: Johns Hopkins University Press, 1976.

―――. *Writing and Difference*. Translated by Alan Bass. Chicago: University of Chicago Press, 1980.

Drabble, Margaret, ed. *The Oxford Companion to English Literature*. Oxford: Oxford University Press, 1985.

Eco, Umberto. *A Theory of Semiotics*. Bloomington: Indiana University Press, 1979.

Engler, Kay. "The Ghostly Lover: The Portrayal of the Animus in *Tristana*." *Anales Galdosianos* 12 (1977): 95–109.

———. *The Structure of Realism: The Novelas Contemporáneas of Benito Pérez Galdós*. Chapel Hill: North Carolina Studies in the Romance Languages and Literatures, 1977.

Feal Deibe, Carlos. "*Tristana* de Galdós: capítulo en la historia de la liberación femenina." *Sin Nombre* 7 (1976): 116–29.

Felman, Shoshana. *Writing and Madness*. Translated by Martha Noel Evans. Ithaca: Cornell University Press, 1985.

Foucault, Michel. *Madness and Civilization: A History of Insanity in the Age of Reason*. Translated by Richard Howard. New York: Random House, 1973.

Friedman, Edward H. " 'Folly and a Woman': Galdós' Rhetoric of Irony in *Tristana*." In *Theory and Practice of Feminist Literary Criticism*, edited by Gabriela Mora and Karen S. Van Hooft, 201–28. Ypsilanti, Mich.: Bilingual Press, 1982.

Garma, Angel. "Jaqueca, seudo-oligofrenia y delirio en un personaje de Pérez Galdós." *Ficción* 14 (1958): 84–102.

Gass, William H. "The Concept of Character in Fiction." In *Fiction and the Figures of Life*, 34–54. New York: Alfred A. Knopf, 1970.

Gillespie, Gerald. "Reality and Fiction in the Novels of Galdós." *Anales Galdosianos* 1 (1966): 11–31.

Gilman, Stephen. "The Birth of Fortunata." *Anales Galdosianos* 1 (1966): 71–83.

———. *Galdós and the Art of the European Novel: 1867–1887*. Princeton: Princeton University Press, 1981.

Girard, René. *Deceit, Desire and the Novel: Self and Other in Literary Structure*. Translated by Yvonne Freccero. Baltimore: Johns Hopkins University Press, 1965.

Glendinning, Nigel. "Psychology and Politics in the First Series of the *Episodios nacionales*." In *Galdós Studies*, edited by J. E. Varey, 36–61. London: Tamesis, 1970.

Gold, Hazel. "From Sensibility to Intelligibility: Transformations in the Spanish Epistolary Novel from Romanticism to Realism." In *La Chispa '85: Selected Proceedings*, edited by Gilbert Paolini, 133–43. New Orleans: Tulane University, 1985.

———. "Problems of Closure in *Fortunata y Jacinta*: Of Narrators, Readers and Their Just Deserts/Desserts." *Neophilologus* 70 (1986): 228–38.

Goldin, David. "Calderón, Cervantes, and Irony in *Tristana*." *Anales Galdosianos* 20 (1985): 97–126.

Guillén, Jorge. *Lenguaje y poesía*. Madrid: Alianza Editorial, 1972.

Gullón, Agnes M. "The Bird Motif and the Introductory Motif: Structure in *Fortunata y Jacinta*." *Anales Galdosianos* 9 (1974): 51–75.

Gullón, Germán. "Narrativizando la historia: *La corte de Carlos IV*." *Anales Galdosianos* 19 (1984): 45–52.

———. *La novela como acto imaginativo*. Madrid: Taurus, 1983.

———. "*Tristana*: literaturización y estructura novelesca." *Hispanic Review* 45 (1977): 13–27.

———. "Unidad de *El doctor Centeno*." *Cuadernos Hispanoamericanos* 250–52 (1970–1971): 579–85.

Gullón, Ricardo. "Los *Episodios*: la primera serie." *Philological Quarterly* 52 (1972): 292–312.

———. "La historia como materia novelable." *Anales Galdosianos* 5 (1970): 23–37.

———. Introducción. In *La incógnita*, by Benito Pérez Galdós, edited by Ricardo Gullón, 7–33. Madrid: Taurus, 1976.

———. Introducción. In *Realidad*, by Benito Pérez Galdós, edited by Ricardo Gullón, 7–30. Madrid: Taurus, 1977.

———. *Técnicas de Galdós*. Madrid: Taurus, 1980.

Haddad, Elaine. "Maximiliano Rubín." *Archivum* 7 (1957): 101–14.

Hafter, Monroe. "Ironic Reprise in Galdós' Novels." *PMLA* 76 (1961): 233–39.

Hinterhäuser, Hans. *Los "Episodios Nacionales" de Benito Pérez Galdós*. Madrid: Editorial Gredos, 1963.

Holmberg, Arthur C. "Louis Lambert and Maximiliano Rubín: The Inner Vision and the Outer Man." *Hispanic Review* 46 (1978): 119–36.

Hutcheon, Linda. *Narcissistic Narrative: The Metafictional Paradox*. New York: Methuen, 1984.

———. *A Theory of Parody: The Teachings of Twentieth-Century Art Forms*. New York: Methuen, 1985.

Innis, Robert E. Introduction to *Semiotics: An Introductory Anthology*, edited by Robert E. Innis, vii-xvi. Bloomington: Indiana University Press, 1985.

Iser, Wolfgang. *The Act of Reading: A Theory of Aesthetic Response*. Baltimore: Johns Hopkins University Press, 1980.

James, Henry. "The Art of Fiction." In *Critical Theory Since Plato*, edited by Hazard Adams, 661–70. New York: Harcourt Brace Jovanovich, 1971.

Kronik, John W. "*El amigo Manso* and the Game of Fictive Autonomy." *Anales Galdosianos* 12 (1977): 71–94.

———. "Galdosian Reflections: Feijoo and the Fabrication of Fortunata." *Modern Language Notes* 97 (1982): 272–310.

———. "Narraciones interiores en *Fortunata y Jacinta*." In *Homenaje a Juan*

López Morillas, edited by José Amor y Vázquez and A. D. Kossoff, 275–91. Madrid: Editorial Castalia, 1982.

Lacan, Jacques. *Écrits*. Translated by Alan Sheridan. New York: W. W. Norton & Company, 1977.

Levin, Harry. *The Gates of Horn: A Study of Five French Realists*. New York: Oxford University Press, 1963.

Lida, Denah. "Galdós, entre crónica y novela." *Anales Galdosianos* 8 (1973): 63–77.

———. "Sobre el 'krausismo' de Galdós." *Anales Galdosianos* 2 (1967): 11–15.

Livingstone, Leon. "Interior Duplication and the Problem of Form in the Modern Spanish Novel." *PMLA* 73 (1958): 393–406.

———. "The Law of Nature and Women's Liberation in *Tristana*." *Anales Galdosianos* 7 (1972): 93–100.

López Muñoz, José Luis. "Felipe Centeno, un héroe oscuro e inédito." *Papeles de Son Armadans* 73 (1974): 249–58.

Lowe, Jennifer. "Age, Illusion and Irony in *Tristana*." *Anales Galdosianos* 29 (1985): 107–11.

Lukács, Georg. *The Historical Novel*. Translated by Hannah Mitchell and Stanley Mitchell. Lincoln: University of Nebraska Press, 1962.

Miller, Beth. "Imagen e ideología en *Tristana* de Galdós." In *Mujeres en la literatura*, 46–50. Mexico City: Fleischer Editora, 1978.

Miró, Emilio. "*Tristana* o la imposibilidad de ser." *Cuadernos Hispanoamericanos* 250–52 (1970–1971): 505–22.

Moi, Toril. *Sexual/Textual Politics: Feminist Literary Theory*. New York: Methuen, 1985.

Montesinos, José F. *Galdós*. Vol 2. Madrid: Editorial Castalia, 1968–1972.

Moreno Castillo, Gloria. "La unidad de tema en *El doctor Centeno*." In *Actas del Primer Congreso Internacional de Estudios Galdosianos*, 382–86. Las Palmas: Excmo. Cabildo Insular de Gran Canaria, 1977.

Newton, Nancy. "*El amigo Manso* and the Relativity of Reality." *Revista de Estudios Hispánicos* 7 (1973): 113–25.

Nimetz, Michael. *Humor in Galdós: A Study of the Novelas contemporáneas*. New Haven: Yale University Press, 1968.

Ostriker, Alicia. "The Thieves of Language: Women Poets and Revisionist Mythmaking." In *The New Feminist Criticism: Essays on Women, Literature, and Theory*, edited by Elaine Showalter, 314–38. New York: Pantheon Books, 1985.

Pardo Bazán, Emilia. "Tristana." In *Obras completas*, edited by Harry L. Kirby, Jr., 3:1119–23. Madrid: Aguilar, 1973.

Peirce, Charles S. "Logic as Semiotic: The Theory of Signs." In *Semiotics:*

An Introductory Anthology, edited by Robert E. Innis, 4–23. Bloomington: Indiana University Press, 1985.

Penuel, Arnold M. "The Ambiguity of Orozco's Virtue in Galdós' *La incógnita* and *Realidad.*" *Hispania* 53 (1970): 411–18.

Pérez Firmat, Gustavo. "Metafiction Again." *Taller Literario* 1 (Fall 1980): 30–38.

Pérez Galdós, Benito. *Ensayos de crítica literaria.* Edited by Laureano Bonet. Barcelona: Ediciones Península, 1972.

―――. *Fortunata and Jacinta.* Translated by Agnes Gullón. Athens: University of Georgia Press, 1986.

―――. *Obras completas (Episodios nacionales).* Edited by Federico C. Sainz de Robles. 2d ed. Vols. 1–2. Madrid: Aguilar, 1986.

―――. *Obras completas (Novelas).* Edited by Federico C. Sainz de Robles. 1st ed. Vols. 1–3. Madrid: Aguilar, 1970–1973.

―――. *Our Friend Manso.* Translated by Robert Russell. New York: Columbia University Press, 1987.

Prince, Gerald. "Introduction to the Study of the Narratee." In *Reader-Response Criticism: From Formalism to Post-Structuralism*, edited by Jane P. Tompkins, 7–25. Baltimore: Johns Hopkins University Press, 1980.

Randolph, E. D. "A Source for Maxi Rubín in *Fortunata y Jacinta.*" *Hispania* 51 (1968): 49–56.

Real Academia Española: Diccionario manual de la lengua española. Madrid: Espasa-Calpe, 1979.

Regalado García, Antonio. *Benito Pérez Galdós y la novela histórica española 1868–1912.* Madrid: Insula, 1966.

Ribbans, Geoffrey. *Fortunata y Jacinta.* London: Grant & Cutler, 1977.

Rodríguez, Alfred. "Ido del Sagrario: notas sobre el otro novelista en Galdós." In *Estudios sobre la novela de Galdós*, 87–103. Madrid: Porrúa, 1978.

―――. *An Introduction to the Episodios Nacionales of Galdós.* New York: Las Américas Publishing Co., 1967.

Rodríguez-Puértolas, Julio. *Galdós: burguesía y revolución.* Madrid: Turner Libros, 1975.

Russell, Robert. "La óptica del novelista en *La incógnita* y *Realidad.*" *Filología* 10 (1964): 179–85.

Sackett, Theodore A. "Creation and Destruction of Personality in *Tristana*: Galdós and Buñuel." *Anales Galdosianos* (extra issue, 1976): 71–90.

Sánchez, Roberto. "Galdós' *Tristana*, Anatomy of a 'Disappointment.'" *Anales Galdosianos* 12 (1977): 110–27.

―――. *El teatro en la novela: Galdós y Clarín.* Madrid: Insula, 1974.

Saussure, Ferdinand de. *Course in General Linguistics.* Translated by Wade Baskin. New York: Philosophical Library, 1959.

Scanlon, Geraldine M. "*El doctor Centeno*: A Study in Obsolescent Values." *Bulletin of Hispanic Studies* 55 (1978): 245–53.

Schmidt, Ruth A. "Tristana and the Importance of Opportunity." *Anales Galdosianos* 9 (1974): 135–44.

Scholes, Robert. *Fabulation and Metafiction*. Urbana: University of Illinois Press, 1979.

Schor, Naomi. "Fiction as Interpretation/Interpretation as Fiction." In *The Reader in the Text: Essays on Audience and Interpretation*, edited by Susan R. Suleiman and Inge Crosman, 165–82. Princeton: Princeton University Press, 1980.

Sieber, Harry. *Language and Society in "La vida de Lazarillo de Tormes."* Baltimore: Johns Hopkins University Press, 1978.

Sieburth, Stephanie. "Interpreting *La Regenta*: Coherence vs. Entropy." *MLN* 102 (1987): 274–91.

Sinnigen, John H. "Resistance and Rebellion in *Tristana*." *MLN* 91 (1976): 277–91.

Sobejano, Gonzalo. "Forma literaria y sensibilidad social en *La incógnita* y *Realidad*, de Galdós." *Revista Hispánica Moderna* 30 (1964): 89–107.

———. "Galdós y el vocabulario de los amantes." *Anales Galdosianos* 1 (1966): 85–100.

Spires, Robert. *Beyond the Metafictional Mode: Directions in the Modern Spanish Novel*. Lexington: University Press of Kentucky, 1984.

Tarrío, Angel. *Lectura semiológica de Fortunata y Jacinta*. Santa Cruz de Tenerife: Excmo. Cabildo Insular de Gran Canaria, 1982.

Todorov, Tzvetan. *The Poetics of Prose*. Translated by Richard Howard. Ithaca: Cornell University Press, 1977.

Turner, Harriet. "The Control of Confusion and Clarity in *El amigo Manso*." *Anales Galdosianos* 15 (1980): 45–61.

Ullman, J. C., and G. H. Allison. "Galdós as Psychiatrist in *Fortunata y Jacinta*." *Anales Galdosianos* 9 (1974): 7–36.

Urbina, Eduardo. "Mesías y redentores: constante estructural y motivo temático en *Fortunata y Jacinta*." *Bulletin Hispanique* 83 (1981): 379–98.

Urey, Diane. "The Confusion and the Fusion of History and Fiction in the Third Series of Galdós' *Episodios Nacionales*." *Philological Quarterly* 64 (1985): 459–73.

———. *Galdós and the Irony of Language*. New York: Cambridge University Press, 1982.

———. "Isabel II and Historical Truth in the Fourth Series of Galdós' *Episodios Nacionales*." *MLN* 98 (1983): 189–207.

———. "Linguistic Mediation in the *Episodios Nacionales* of Galdós: *Vergara*." *Philological Quarterly* 62 (1983): 263–71.

———. *The Novel Histories of Galdós*. Princeton: Princeton University Press, 1989.

Utt, Roger L. " 'El pájaro voló': observaciones sobre un leitmotif en *Fortunata y Jacinta.*" *Anales Galdosianos* 9 (1974): 37–50.

Valis, Noël M. "Art, Memory, and the Human in Galdós' *Tristana.*" *Kentucky Romance Quarterly* 31 (1984): 207–20.

Waugh, Patricia. *Metafiction: The Theory and Practice of Self-Conscious Fiction.* New York: Methuen, 1984.

White, Hayden. *The Content of the Form: Narrative Discourse and Historical Representation.* Baltimore: Johns Hopkins University Press, 1987.

———. *Metahistory: The Historical Imagination in Nineteenth-Century Europe.* Baltimore: Johns Hopkins University Press, 1973.

Wilde, Oscar. "The Decay of Lying." In *Critical Theory Since Plato*, edited by Hazard Adams, 673–86. New York: Harcourt Brace Jovanovich, 1971.

Index

Alas, Leopoldo (Clarín): as critic, 63n19, 100; *La Regenta,* 2, 132–33
Alcázar, Baltasar de, 61n15
Alter, Robert, 4, 39n5
Altman, Janet, 89
Anderson, Farris, 57n10
Andreu, Alicia, 93n16, 129n1
Aristotle, *Poetics,* 98n24
Auerbach, Erich, 107n3
Autobiography, fictional, 9, 109–10, 113, 128

Bakhtin, Mikhail, 129
Barthes, Roland, 1, 5, 12, 15, 33, 35, 36n3, 42n11, 48, 57n9, 63, 105, 115n15, 126, 130, 132, 133
Benveniste, Emile, 115n15, 127–28
Bly, Peter, 128n21
Borges, Jorge Luis, 133
Bosch, Rafael, 4n10
Boyd, Michael, 4
Burke, Kenneth, 21n21

Casalduero, Joaquín, 14n4
Cervantes, Miguel de, *Don Quixote,* 45, 46, 61, 63n18, 89, 105n34, 121, 125
Chamberlin, Vernon, 29n29
Conventions: general discussion of, 1, 128; linguistic, 15, 68; literary, 58–59, 68, 86, 115; and realism, 5, 33, 131
Correa, Gustavo, 50n18
Culler, Jonathan, 5, 9n24, 16n11, 130–31

Dante Alighieri, *Inferno,* 59, 68
Dendle, Brian, 107, 110
Derrida, Jacques, 99n25
Detective novel, 95n18
Dialogue novel, 9, 100–104
Don Quixote. See Cervantes, Miguel de

Eco, Umberto, 3, 5n19, 88
Education, 16, 40
Engler, Kay, 4, 11, 56–57n7
Epistolary novel, 9, 10, 84, 89

Feal Deibe, Carlos, 56n2
Felman, Shoshana, 14n2, 33, 34
Feminism, 55–57, 64, 67, 71–72, 75, 79. *See also* Woman
Flaubert, Gustave: 132–33; *Madame Bovary,* 2
Folletín (serial novel), 24n24, 43, 91–95, 101
Foucault, Michel, 30n30
Friedman, Edward, 56

Gass, William, 57n9, 62n17
Gillespie, Gerald, 101n29
Gilman, Stephen, 14n4
Girard, René, 17, 86
Glendinning, Nigel, 107n2
Gold, Hazel, 85n6, 132n6
Goldin, David, 61n16
Guillén, Jorge, *Lenguaje y poesía,* 70n25
Gullón, Germán, 2n4, 19n18, 36n2, 48, 60n14, 68, 78, 108n8
Gullón, Ricardo, 6n21, 11, 29, 83n5, 86n8, 94n17, 108, 124

Haddad, Elaine, 21n22
Hafter, Monroe, 82
Hinterhäuser, Hans, 107
History (historical discourse, historical novel), 10, 106–9, 115n15, 124–28
Holmberg, Arthur, 14n4
Hutcheon, Linda, 1–2, 5–6, 15, 16n13, 37, 131

Innis, Robert, 2
Iser, Wolfgang, 12n28

James, Henry: "The Figure in the Carpet," 105n36; "The Art of Fiction," 130

Kronik, John, 6, 15n7, 16n12, 20n20, 40n8, 43n12

Lacan, Jacques, 29n29
Levin, Harry, 64n19
Lida, Denah, 40n7, 94n17
Livingstone, Leon, 56n2, 82n3
López Muñoz, José Luis, 46n14, 50n18
Lowe, Jennifer, 66n20
Lukács, Georg, 107

Madame Bovary. See Flaubert, Gustave
Madness: in literature, 34; in Maximiliano Rubín, 9, 13–15, 17, 22–33
Memoirs. *See* Autobiography, fictional
Metafiction, 4–5, 15, 131. *See also* Self-consciousness
Metalanguage, 3, 42, 128
Miller, Beth, 56n2
Mimesis, 1–2, 54. *See also* Realism
Miró, Emilio, 56, 67n21
Moi, Toril, 18n17, 29n29
Montesinos, José, 14–15n5, 36n2
Moratín, Leandro Fernández de, *El sí de las niñas,* 111–12
Moreno Castillo, Gloria, 36n2

Names (naming), 48–49, 60, 62–63, 115–16, 118, 126
Narratee, 89–91
Newton, Nancy, 6n21, 96n19
Nimetz, Michael, 78n30

Orbajosa, 10–11

Pardo Bazán, Emilia, 55–56
Parody, 37–38
Peirce, Charles, 41
Penuel, Arnold, 103n32
Pérez Firmat, Gustavo, 6n21
Pérez Galdós, Benito:
—Characters: Albrit, Conde de, 101–2n30; Amaranta, 113–15, 118–20; Anselmo, Don (*La sombra*), 10; Araceli, Gabriel de, 109–28; Ballester, Segismundo, 29–30,

53–54; Bringas, Rosalía de (Rosalía Pipaón de la Barca), 39; Cadalso, Luisito, 22n23; Cadalso, Víctor, 43; Carlos IV, 113; Centeno, Felipe, 35–54, 132; Cisneros, Augusta: in *La incógnita,* 84–86; in *Realidad,* 97n21, 101; Delgado, Jesús, 40, 48, 49; Díaz, Horacio, 64–77 passim; Equis X, 81, 89–92, 99–100, 104–5; Fernando VII, 113, 127; Fly, Athenais (Miss Fly), 122–23, 126; Fortunata, 16, 18–23, 26–31, 57; Godoy, Manuel, 113; González, Pepa (Pepita), 110–11; Gray, Lord, 121; Ido del Sagrario, José, 23, 24n24, 52–53; Ido del Sagrario, Rosa, 48; Inés (de Santorcaz), 116–18; Infante, Manolo, 39; Irene, 7; Isabel, Doña *(El doctor Centeno),* 46; Jacinta (Arnaiz y Cordero), 16, 43; Lesbia *(La corte de Carlos IV),* 118–19; López Garrido, Don Juan (Lope Garrido), 60–64, 78; Lupe, Doña, 20; Máiquez, Isidoro, 118–19; Malibrán, Cornelio, 96; Manso, Máximo, 6–7, 59, 77, 88n9, 132; Miquis, Alejandro *(El doctor Centeno),* 35–36, 45–51, 52; Orozco, Tomás *(Realidad),* 103–4; Paca, Doña (Francisca Juárez, *Misericordia*), 39; Peña, Manolo, 6–7, 41n9; Polo, Pedro *(El doctor Centeno),* 35–36, 41–45, 48, 51; Ponce *(Fortunata y Jacinta),* 53; Rey, Pepe, 10–11; Rubín, Maximiliano, 13–34, 39, 50, 51, 53, 65; Rumblar family, 120–21; Samaniego, Aurora *(Fortunata y Jacinta),* 27–28, 29; Santa Cruz, Juanito, 16, 27, 43; Saturna *(Tristana),* 64; Socorro, Juanito del, 42–44; Solís, Josefina, 60–61; Torquemada, Francisco, 41n9; Tristana, 56–79; Viera, Federico *(Realidad),* 101–3
—Works: *El abuelo,* 100n27, 101–2n30; *El amigo Manso,* 6–7, 59, 76n27, 77, 88n9; *Bailén,* 124; *La batalla de los Arapiles,* 122–23, 126, 127; *Cádiz,* 120–21; *La corte de Carlos IV,* 109–19 passim, 127; *La de*

Bringas, 39; *El doctor Centeno,* 9, 35–54; *Doña Perfecta,* 10–11; *Episodios nacionales,* 10, 106–28; *Fortunata y Jacinta,* 9, 13–34; *Gerona,* 127; *La incógnita,* 10, 39, 80, 81–105, 132; *Miau,* 22n23, 39, 43; *Misericordia,* 39; *Napoleón, en Chamartín,* 120, 125; *El 19 de marzo y el 2 de mayo,* 117; "Observaciones sobre la novela contemporánea en España," 97n22, 122–23n17; *Realidad,* 81–83, 99–105; *La sombra,* 10; *Torquemada en el purgatorio,* 41n; *Trafalgar,* 115–16, 127; *Tristana,* 10, 55–80
Prince, Gerald, 89n12

Realism: 1, 36, 53–54; and self-consciousness, 3–5, 130–34
Referential illusion (reality effect), 5, 33, 36, 115n15. *See also* Conventions and realism
Regalado García, Antonio, 107
La Regenta. See Alas, Leopoldo
Rodríguez, Alfred, 107
Rodríguez-Puértolas, Julio, 17n14
Romanticism, 50–51, 66–67, 70, 71
Russell, Robert, 82

Sackett, Theodore, 56–57
Sánchez, Roberto, 56, 100–101
Saussure, Ferdinand de, 2–3, 14n3
Scanlon, Geraldine, 36n2, 40n7
Schmidt, Ruth, 56n2

Scholes, Robert, 4
Schor, Naomi, 15
Self-consciousness (self-referentiality or self-reflexivity): and (nineteenth-century) realism, 3–5, 130–34; in Galdós, 5–12
Semiotics (as discipline), 1–3
Serial novel. *See Folletín*
Shakespeare, William: *Hamlet,* 72; *Othello,* 112, 118–19
El sí de las niñas. See Moratín, Leandro Fernández de
Sieber, Harry, 109n10
Sieburth, Stephanie, 2n4
Sinnigen, John, 78n31
Sobejano, Gonzalo, 68n22, 102n31

Tarrío, Angel, 104n33
Todorov, Tzvetan, 95n18, 105n36
Turner, Harriet, 6n21

Urbina, Eduardo, 17n14
Urey, Diane, 7n23, 11, 79n32, 82, 85n6, 106n1, 108n6, 109n9

Valis, Noël, 55n1, 57n7

Waugh, Patricia, 4–5
White, Hayden, 108
Wilde, Oscar, "The Decay of Lying," 98
Woman, 17–18, 55–57, 64–65, 67, 71–72, 75, 79, 116–17. *See also* Feminism